CW01659182

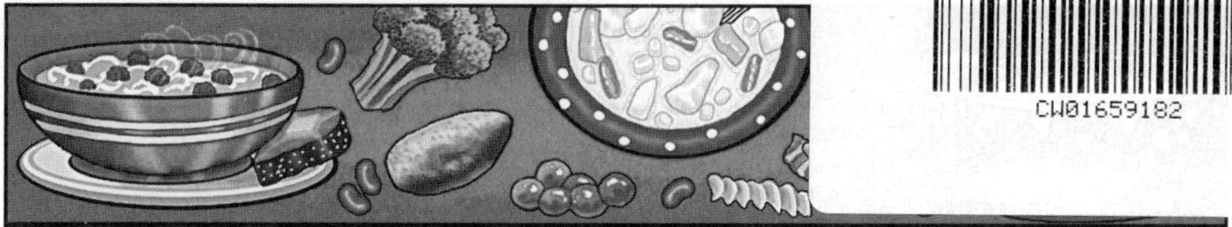

365 Easy Soup Recipes

Simple, delicious soups and stews to warm the heart

HINKLER BOOKS

Cover by Nancy Bohanan
Pre-press by Graphic Print Group

365 Easy Soup Recipes
Published in 2009 by Hinkler Books Pty Ltd
45–55 Fairchild Street
Heatherton VIC 3202 Australia
www.hinklerbooks.com

© Cookbook Resources, LLC 2008

10 9 8 7 6 5 4 3 2
14 13 12 11 10

All rights reserved. No part of this publication may be reproduced, stored in a retrieval system, or transmitted in any way or by any means, electronic, mechanical, photocopying, recording or otherwise, without the prior written permission of the copyright holders.

ISBN: 978 1 7418 3130 6
Printed and bound in China

Introduction

Nothing says home and comfort more than a big pot of homemade soup simmering gently on the stove. Soups and stews are one of life's great comforts. They are warming, aromatic, brimming with flavour and bring back sweet memories of mum's chicken noodle soup, the one soup that always seemed to make even the worst cold vanish. There's just something about soup that makes everything seem better.

Thick or thin, hot or cold, subtle or spicy, brothy or chunky, *365 Easy Soup Recipes* has a soup to fit any mood and every taste. From cover to cover simple delicious recipes can help make family meals into 'feel-good' meals. These soups, stews, chillies and chowders are family favourites and help build family traditions.

Warm your kitchen and your heart with **Zesty Creamy Chicken Soup**, a surprisingly easy recipe for a fast chicken soup. Or try a big rich bowl of **Incredible Broccoli-Cheese Soup**. And it doesn't get any easier than **Easy Chunky Chilli**, chock-full of beefy stew meat, vegetables and spices. Our collection of recipes for soups and stews makes it possible for you to ladle up a bowl of soup every day of the year!

Cooking is one of life's simple pleasures. And these recipes make it easy to enjoy quality time with people you care about.

Contents

Contents

Contents

Simmering Soups for Centuries

Our prehistoric ancestors, who were forced to stalk and kill their dinner before they could even think about cooking it, discovered how to mingle meats and vegetables with water before there was even a pot or kettle to cook them in! They did it for survival – a way to feed the old and toothless members of their tribes.

Fossil remains of elderly Neanderthal people were found in France with teeth worn down below gum level. They could only have been kept alive through the compassion of tribe members who found a food alternative to indigestible plants and tough meats.

Historians believe that humans knew how to boil well before 6,000 B.C. when earthenware pottery was discovered. Prehistoric humans found that reptile shells and animal hides made perfect vessels to boil liquid filled with fresh meat.

Evidence including residue sticking to pots indicates that our ancestors were regularly eating soup by the Bronze and Iron Ages.

The origins of the word 'soup' go back to broth. Deriving from Old English, broth served over bread in a bowl was called 'sop' or 'sup'. From this, the word 'soup' evolved. In French, it is 'soupe', in Spanish, 'sopa', and in Dutch, 'soep'. In English, it's soup and we've created *365 Easy Soup Recipes* just for you.

Who's Who: Soups, Stews, Chowders and Chillies

Soups & Stews

Most of us have a pretty good idea of the difference between soups and stews. **Soups are thin and stews are thick.** But if you want to know more about these comforting dishes, read on to find out many other differences.

Soups

Soups start with liquid, usually hot water. Meats, beans and vegetables are boiled to extract the flavours of the ingredients and that is the broth or stock used as the base. As they boil they break down and mix with the liquid for a distinctive blend of flavours.

Clear Soups

Clear soups are called broth, bouillon or consomme. **Purees** are mixes of vegetables and liquid thickened by the starch in the vegetables. Other types of purees are thickened with cream, milk, eggs, rice, flour or grains.

Stews

Stews are very similar to **soups** because they are combinations of vegetables and meats cooked in a broth or stock. The ingredients are much the same as **soups**. **Stews** usually have larger pieces of meat and vegetables than do **soups**. These large pieces are boiled, covered and simmered for a long time to tenderise the ingredients.

Stews are usually served as a main course and **soups** are usually served as a first course. **Stews** are usually heartier and more filling than **soups**, but there is little difference in the popularity of both.

Chowders

Chowders are similar to stews, but mainly consist of fish or clams, potatoes and onions. New England clam **chowder** has a cream base and Manhattan clam **chowder** has a tomato base. There is also corn **chowder** with a cream base.

Chilli

Chilli refers to the state dish of Texas, where it originated. Dallas's Frank X. Tolbert, founder of the International Terlingua Chilli Cook-off and chilli aficionado, called **chilli** 'a bowl of red' to reflect the proper colour of the dish.

Dedication

With a mission of helping you bring family and friends to the table, this book aims to make family meals and cooking for friends simple, easy and delicious.

We recognise the importance of a meal together as a means of building family bonds with memories and traditions that will be treasured for a lifetime. It is an opportunity to sit down with each other and share more than food.

This cookbook is dedicated with gratitude and respect to all those who show their love with homecooked meals, bringing family and friends to the table.

More and more statistical studies are finding that family meals play a significant role in childhood development. Children who eat with their families four or more nights per week are healthier, attain higher marks at school, score higher on aptitude tests and are less likely to have problems with drugs.

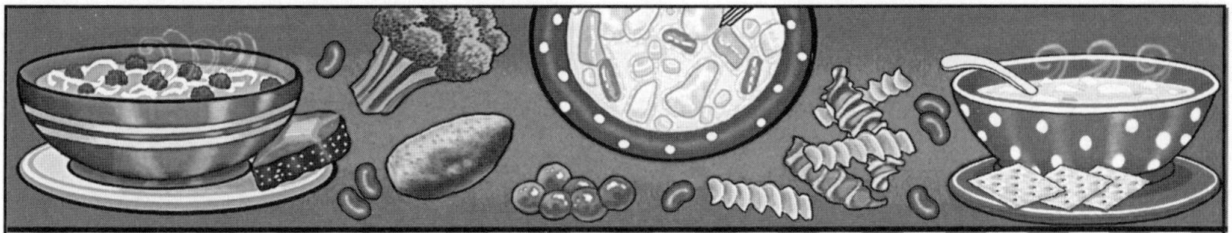

Satisfying Summer Soups

Try one of these light fruit or veggie soups to refresh your senses on a hot summer's day.

Satisfying Summer Soups Contents

Check seasonings of cold soups just before serving because chilled foods tend to dull the taste buds and will need more seasoning than hot soups.

Cold Peach Soup

This is a beautiful and delicious soup to serve as a first course at a luncheon or gathering of friends.

680 g (1½ pounds) fresh peaches, peeled, sliced
1 230-g (8-ounce) carton sour cream
1 230-g (8-ounce) carton peach yoghurt
2½ cups (625 ml) orange juice
1 tablespoon (15 ml) lemon juice
3 tablespoons (40 g) sugar

- Puree peaches in blender or food processor until smooth. Add sour cream, yoghurt, orange juice and lemon juice and process until they blend well. Stir in sugar, cover and refrigerate for at least 2 hours. Serves 8.

Edna Earle's Cold Peach Soup

This is delicious for summer luncheons with vegetables or chicken-salad sandwiches.

910 g (2 pounds) peaches
1 tablespoon (15 ml) lemon juice
3 tablespoons (50 g) quick-cooking tapioca (or sago)
3 tablespoons (40 g) sugar
¾ cup orange cordial

- Puree peaches with lemon juice and set aside. Combine tapioca, sugar, a little salt and 1 cup (250 ml) water in saucepan. Heat to full boil and stir constantly until mixture thickens.
- Transfer to medium bowl. Stir in orange cordial. Add 1½ cups (375 ml) water and stir until smooth. Mix in pureed peaches, cover and refrigerate. Serve cold. Serves 8.

TIP: Make this soup ahead of time so it has time to chill.

Luncheon Fruit Soup

¾ cup (150 g) sugar
4 tablespoons (70 g) quick-cooking tapioca (or sago)
¼ teaspoon (1 ml) ground cinnamon
¾ cup orange cordial
2 cups (310 g) sliced peaches
1 425-g (15-ounce) can pear slices with juice
1 230-g (8-ounce) can crushed pineapple with juice
455 g (16 ounces) strawberries, thawed, sliced

- Combine sugar, tapioca, cinnamon and 3 cups (750 ml) water in large saucepan. Cook over medium heat and stir constantly for about 10 minutes or until mixture thickens. Remove from heat and pour in orange cordial.
- Cut peaches and pears into bite-size pieces. Stir peaches, pears, pineapple and strawberries into tapioca-orange mixture. Cover and refrigerate for at least 2 hours. Serves 8.

Pat's Chilled Strawberry Soup

560 g (20 ounces) strawberries
½ cup (50 g) cranberries
460 g (16 ounces) strawberry yoghurt

- Combine all ingredients in blender and mix until smooth.
- Refrigerate for 1 to 2 hours before serving. Serves 4.

Cold Strawberry Soup

2¼ cups (405 g) strawberries
⅓ cup (70 g) sugar
½ cup (120 g) sour cream
½ cup (125 ml) pouring cream
½ cup (125 ml) light red wine

- Puree strawberries and sugar in blender. Pour into pitcher, stir in sour cream and cream and blend well.
- Add red wine and 1¼ cups (310 ml) water. Stir and refrigerate before serving. Serves 4 to 6.

For cold soups, chill your soup bowls so that the soup remains cold longer.

Chilled Summertime Soup

3 cups (530 g) chilled, cubed fresh cantaloupe
3 cups (530 g) chilled, cubed fresh honeydew melon
2 cups (500 ml) chilled, fresh orange juice
2 cups (500 ml) chilled, white wine or sparkling
¼ cup (60 ml) chilled, fresh lime juice
3 tablespoons (65 g) honey

- Puree 2 cups (355 g) cantaloupe in food processor or blender and pour into large bowl. Puree honeydew melon and combine with pureed cantaloupe, orange juice, white wine and lime juice.
- Pour in honey and mix well. Chop remaining cantaloupe and add to bowl. Serve immediately. Serves 8.

TIP: Fresh mint as garnish is always a nice touch.

Strawberry-Orange Soup

1½ cups (270 g) fresh strawberries
1 cup (250 ml) orange juice
¼ cup (85 g) honey
½ cup (120 g) sour cream
½ cup (125 ml) white wine

- Combine all ingredients in blender and puree.
- Chill thoroughly. Stir before pouring into individual soup bowls. Serves 4.

Chilled Yoghurt Soups

Here are two light, chilled soups that are great. Yoghurt has a unique flavour and gives soups a delicious, tangy taste. Both of these soups are prepared the same way, but one uses cucumber and one uses avocados.

Chilled Yoghurt Soup with Cucumbers

4 cucumbers, peeled, seeded
3 cups (680 g) plain yoghurt
1 tablespoon (15 ml) minced onion

- Place 3 cucumbers, yoghurt and onion in food processor or blender and process until just smooth. Add a little salt, cover and refrigerate for several hours.
- Chill soup bowls at the same time and pour soup into bowls when ready to serve. Thinly slice remaining cucumber and garnish soup with several slices. Serves 4.

Chilled Yoghurt Soup with Avocados

4 ripe avocados, peeled, seeded
3 cups (680 g) plain yoghurt
1 tablespoon (15 ml) minced onion

- Place 3 avocados, yoghurt and onion in food processor or blender and process until just smooth. Add a little salt, cover and refrigerate for several hours.
- Chill soup bowls at the same time and pour soup into bowls when ready to serve. Thinly slice remaining avocado and garnish soup with several slices. Serves 4.

Summer Breeze Raspberry Soup

3½ cups (430 g) fresh raspberries
1 cup (250 ml) rose wine
¾ cup (150 g) sugar
230 g (8 ounces) sour cream

- Mash raspberries in bowl, mix in blender and strain to remove seeds. Add enough water to make 3½ cups (875 ml). Place raspberry mixture, wine, sugar and a little salt in saucepan.
- Bring to a boil, reduce heat, cover and simmer for 5 minutes. Cool, add sour cream and stir until it blends thoroughly. Refrigerate for about 4 hours. Serves 6.

Easy Gazpacho

2 795-g (28-ounce) cans diced tomatoes
1 seedless cucumber, peeled, cubed
1 cup (160 g) chopped red onion
1 cup (100 g) chopped celery
2 hot green chillies, seeded, coarsely chopped

- Work in batches to combine all ingredients plus a little salt and pepper in food processor and pulse until mixture is thick.
- Garnish with several lemon slices, if desired. Serves 8.

TIP: Wear rubber gloves when removing seeds from chillies.

White Gazpacho

¼ cup (60 ml) packed parsley leaves
3 cloves garlic, chopped
1 teaspoon dried basil
1 teaspoon dried oregano
3 seedless cucumbers, peeled, chopped
1 green capsicum, seeded, quartered
1 white onion, quartered
2 230-g (8-ounce) cartons plain yoghurt
1 litre carton chicken stock
2 tablespoons (30 ml) lemon juice
Hot sauce

- Finely chop parsley and add garlic, basil and oregano in bowl. Place cucumbers, capsicum and onion in blender, process until coarsely chopped and add parsley mixture.
- Stir in yoghurt, stock, lemon juice and ½ teaspoon each of salt and pepper and mix well. Season to taste with hot sauce and refrigerate. Serves 6.

Rio Grande Gazpacho

This spicy vegetable soup made from a puree of raw vegetables is served cold and is great in summer.

1 cucumber, peeled, seeded, quartered
1 capsicum, seeded, quartered
½ onion, quartered
1 teaspoon (5 ml) minced garlic
2 teaspoons (10 ml) chopped fresh parsley
3¼ cups (810 ml) tomato juice
450 g (1 pound) tomatoes, peeled, quartered, cored
¼ cup (30 g) sliced pimento-stuffed olives
3 tablespoons (45 ml) red wine vinegar
1 tablespoon (15 ml) olive oil
½ teaspoon ground cumin
½ teaspoon oregano
2 teaspoons hot sauce

- Combine cucumber, capsicum, onion, garlic, parsley and 2 cups (500 ml) tomato juice in blender. Process until vegetables are coarsely chopped. Add tomatoes and process again until vegetables are finely chopped.

- Pour into medium container with tight lid. Stir in olives, wine vinegar, olive oil, ½ teaspoon salt, cumin, oregano and hot sauce.

- Stir in remaining tomato juice, cover and refrigerate for 24 hours. Serve cold. Serves 6.

Gazpacho

2 large ripe tomatoes, chopped, drained
1 onion, finely chopped
1 seedless cucumber, peeled, chopped
1 teaspoon (5 ml) minced garlic
200 g (7 ounces) roasted red capsicums, drained
1 1.4-L (48-ounce) can tomato juice
¼ cup (60 ml) lime juice
¼ cup (60 ml) red wine vinegar
2 tablespoons (30 ml) olive oil
½ teaspoon sugar
1 teaspoon hot sauce

- Process tomatoes, onion, cucumber, garlic and roasted red capsicums in food processor or blender.
- Stir puree, tomato juice, lime juice, vinegar, oil, sugar, hot sauce and a little salt and pepper. Cover and refrigerate for at least 4 hours. Serves 8.

Cucumber Dill Soup

3 medium cucumbers, peeled, seeded, cubed
½-litre (14-ounce) carton chicken stock
1 230-g (8-ounce) carton sour cream
3 tablespoons (45 ml) fresh chives, minced
2 teaspoons fresh dill, minced

- Combine cucumbers, 1 cup (250 ml) chicken stock and a little salt in blender. Cover and process until smooth. Transfer to medium bowl and stir in remaining chicken stock.
- Whisk in sour cream, chives and dill. Cover and refrigerate before serving. Garnish with a sprig of dill. Serves 6.

Vichyssoise

¼ cup (60 g) butter
1 onion, chopped
3 medium potatoes, peeled, sliced
1 litre carton chicken stock
2 cups (500 ml) milk
250 ml (8 ounces) pouring cream

- Melt butter and sauté onion in large soup pot. Add sliced potatoes and chicken stock and bring to boil. Reduce heat and simmer about 35 minutes or until potatoes are tender.
- Place about half soup mixture in blender, process until smooth and return to soup pot. Repeat with remaining soup mixture. Stir constantly and add milk, ½ teaspoon pepper and a little salt. Cover and heat on medium until thoroughly hot. Cool.
- Stir in cream, cover and refrigerate. Serve in chilled individual bowls or cover and refrigerate up to 24 hours. Serves 6.

TIP: A parsley garnish is a nice touch, but not a 'must'.

Written soup recipes date from the Middle Ages. There are several soup recipes in a book assembled by the cooks of King Richard II's court in the late 14th century.

Artichoke Soup

3 tablespoons (40 g) butter
2 tablespoons (10 g) finely minced spring onions
1½ tablespoons (10 g) flour
1 litre carton chicken stock
1 455-g (16-ounce) can artichoke bottoms, drained
1 cup (250 ml) unthickened cream

- Melt butter in large saucepan and sauté spring onions. Stir in flour and cook for 3 minutes. Slowly add stock, stir constantly and cook on medium heat until mixture thickens.
- Puree artichokes in blender and stir into stock mixture plus a little salt and pepper. Add cream and heat just until soup is thoroughly hot.
- This soup may be served hot or cold; therefore, when serving cold, do not heat after adding cream. Refrigerate for 2 hours before serving. Serves 6.

Asparagus Chiller

1 280-g (10-ounce) can cream of asparagus soup
⅔ cup (160 g) sour cream
½ cup (60 g) finely chopped cucumber
2 tablespoons (20 g) chopped red onion

- Blend soup, sour cream and ¾ soup can water in bowl. Stir in cucumber and onion.
- Refrigerate for at least 4 hours and serve in chilled bowls. Serves 4.

Chilled Cucumber Soup

2 seedless cucumbers, peeled
½ cup (125 ml) buttermilk*
½ cup (120 g) sour cream
2 teaspoons (10 ml) white vinegar
1 teaspoon olive oil
1 teaspoon sugar
½ teaspoon dried dill, crumbled

- Coarsely chop cucumbers and place cucumbers and ¼ cup (60 ml) buttermilk in blender or food processor and puree. Transfer to bowl and whisk in remaining ingredients with a little salt and pepper.
- Cover bowl, refrigerate for 30 minutes and stir occasionally. Serve in chilled bowls. Serves 4.

**TIP:* *To make buttermilk, mix 1 cup (250 ml) milk with 1 tablespoon (15 ml) lemon juice or vinegar and let milk stand for about 10 minutes.*

Easy Yoghurt-Cucumber Chiller

500 ml (1 pint) carton plain yoghurt
1 cup (250 ml) chicken stock
1 lemon
¾ cup (90 g) peeled, seeded, grated cucumber
¼ cup (60 ml) pouring cream
1 teaspoon finely chopped spring onion with tops
½ teaspoon chopped fresh dill

- Add yoghurt to chicken stock in large bowl and mix well. Cut lemon in half and squeeze 1 teaspoon juice into stock mixture. Cut very thin slices from other half and refrigerate.
- Add remaining ingredients with a little salt and pepper and stir until soup blends well. Refrigerate for at least 4 hours. Before serving, place 1 slice lemon on top of each serving. Serves 8.

Quick Borscht

1 425-g (15-ounce) jar whole red beets
½ litre (14 ounces) carton beef stock
¼ cup (60 g) sour cream

- Drain beets and save liquid. Chop beets and combine with beet liquid and stock in saucepan. Heat for 10 minutes.
- Refrigerate and serve with dollop of sour cream. Serves 4.

Creamy Cucumber Soup

2 seedless cucumbers, peeled, coarsely chopped
2 spring onions, coarsely chopped
1 tablespoon (15 ml) lemon juice
500 ml (1 pint) unthickened cream
230 g (8 ounces) sour cream
1 teaspoon dried dill

- Process cucumbers, onions and lemon juice in blender until mixture is smooth. Transfer pureed mixture to bowl with lid.
- Gently stir in cream, sour cream, dill, 1 teaspoon salt and ½ teaspoon pepper. Add a dash of hot sauce, if you like.
- Cover and refrigerate for several hours before serving. Stir mixture well before serving in soup bowls. Serves 6.

Sweet Carrot Soup

455 g (16 ounces) carrots, shredded
1 cup (250 ml) orange juice
1 cup (250 ml) apricot nectar
¼ cup (60 ml) lemon juice
⅓ cup (115 g) honey
⅓ cup (80 g) sour cream

- Combine carrots, orange juice, apricot nectar and ½ cup (125 ml) water in large saucepan. Bring to boil, reduce heat and simmer for 20 minutes.
- Add lemon juice, honey and sour cream and stir well. Serve soup at room temperature or chilled. Serves 6.

Fresh Avocado Soup

3 ripe avocados
4 tablespoons (60 ml) fresh lemon juice
1 cup (250 ml) chicken stock
230 g (8 ounces) plain yoghurt
Chopped chives

- Peel avocados, remove seeds and cut into pieces. Immediately put avocados, lemon juice, stock and yoghurt into blender and process until smooth.
- Add a little salt and pepper and refrigerate for several hours. Serve in soup bowls with chopped chives on top. Serves 4 to 6.

Avocado-Cream Soup

4 large, ripe avocados, peeled, diced
1½ cups (375 ml) pouring cream
1 litre carton chicken stock
¼ cup (60 ml) dry sherry

- Puree 2 avocados and half cream in blender. Repeat with remaining avocados and cream.
- Bring chicken stock to boil, reduce heat and stir in avocado puree. Add 1 teaspoon (5 ml) salt and sherry and chill thoroughly. Serve in chilled soup bowls. Serves 6.

Chilled Squash Soup

910 g (2 pounds) yellow squash, thinly sliced
1 onion, chopped
½ litre (14 ounces) carton chicken stock
230 g (8 ounces) cream cheese, softened

- Combine squash, onion and stock in saucepan and bring to boil. Cover, reduce heat and simmer for 10 minutes or until tender. Set aside until slightly cool.
- Spoon half squash mixture and half cream cheese into blender. Process until smooth and stop once to scrape down sides. Repeat procedure.
- Stir in a little salt and pepper and refrigerate. Serves 6.

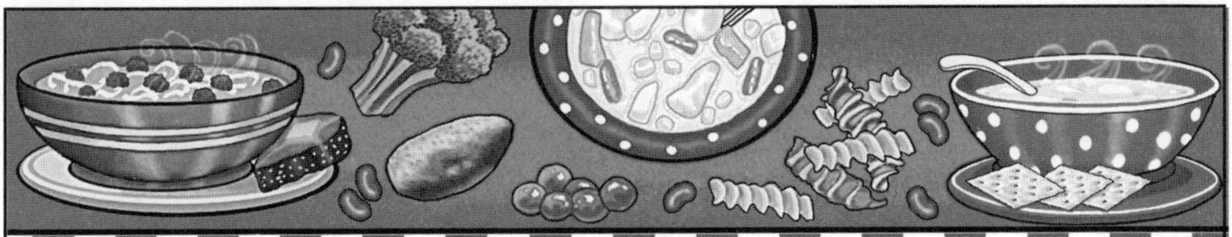

Chicken Chill Chasers

Simple, feel-better recipes for soups, stews, chillies and chowders to chase away the blahs.

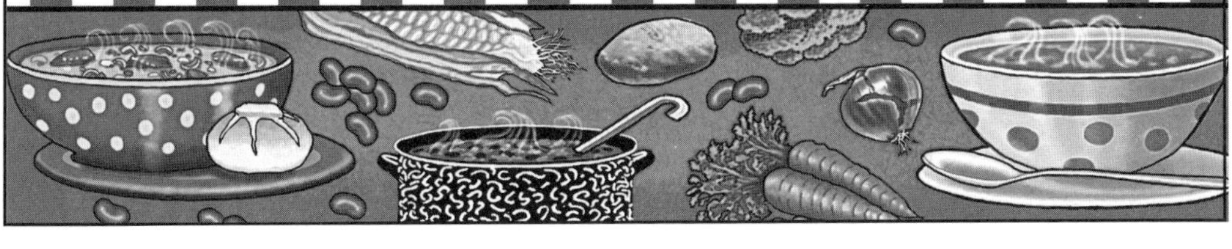

Chicken Chill Chasers Contents

County's Best Chicken Soup

4 boneless, skinless chicken breast halves
1½ litres chicken stock
2 tablespoons (30 g) butter
3 medium new (red) potatoes, cut into wedges
2 sticks celery, chopped
1 carrot, peeled, shredded
280 g (10 ounces) frozen green peas
280 g (10 ounces) frozen corn
1½ cups (375 ml) buttermilk
½ cup (60 g) flour
½ teaspoon cayenne pepper
1 teaspoon Worcestershire sauce

- Bring chicken and stock to a boil in large saucepan and cook for 10 minutes or until done. Remove chicken with slotted spoon and save broth. Cut chicken into bite-size pieces.
- Melt butter in soup pot, add potatoes and cook for about 10 minutes. Add reserved broth, chicken, celery, carrot, peas and corn and simmer for 30 minutes.
- Stir buttermilk and flour until smooth, add to chicken-potato mixture and cook, stirring constantly for 5 minutes. Stir in cayenne pepper and Worcestershire sauce. Serves 8.

All-American Soup

3 boneless, skinless chicken breast halves, cut into strips
1 onion, chopped
Olive oil
1 280-g (10-ounce) can tomatoes
2 chopped green chillies
1 litre carton chicken stock
3 large baking potatoes, peeled, cubed
1 280-g (10-ounce) can cream of celery soup
1 cup (250 ml) milk
1 teaspoon dried basil
230 g (8 ounces) shredded cheddar cheese
½ cup (120 g) sour cream

- Brown and cook chicken strips and onion in large saucepan with a little oil for about 10 minutes.
- Add tomatoes, green chillies, chicken stock and cubed potatoes. Boil and cook for 15 minutes or until potatoes are tender.
- Stir in soup, milk, basil and 1 teaspoon salt. Cook on medium heat and stir constantly until thoroughly hot.
- Stir in cheese until cheese melts. Remove from heat and stir in sour cream. Serves 8.

Creamy Broccoli-Rice Soup

170 g (6 ounces) instant chicken-flavoured rice
280 g (10 ounces) frozen chopped broccoli florets
2 280-g (10-ounce) cans cream of chicken soup
1 340-g (12-ounce) can chicken breast chunks

- Combine rice mix, contents of seasoning packet and 5 cups (1.2 L) water in soup pot. Bring to boil, reduce heat and simmer for 15 minutes.
- Stir in broccoli, chicken soup and chicken. Cover and simmer for additional 5 minutes. Serves 8.

Chicken-Veggie Soup

1 litre carton chicken stock
2 small carrots, thinly sliced
1 stick celery, diced
1 baby leek, halved lengthwise, sliced
1 230-g (8-ounce) can green peas
1 cup (165 g) cooked rice
1 cup (140 g) cooked, sliced chicken
2 teaspoons chopped fresh tarragon

- Pour stock in large saucepan and add carrots, celery and leek. Bring to boil, reduce heat and simmer, partially covered, for 10 minutes.
- Stir in peas, rice and chicken and continue cooking for 10 to 15 minutes or until vegetables are tender. Add chopped tarragon and a little salt and pepper. Serves 8.

Zesty Creamy Chicken Soup

This is a really easy way to whip up a fast chicken soup.

2 tablespoons (30 g) butter
½ onion, finely chopped
1 carrot, grated
1 280-g (10-ounce) can cream of celery soup
1 280-g (10-ounce) can cream of mushroom soup
1 280-g (10-ounce) can cream of chicken soup
½ litre (14 ounces) carton chicken stock
2 soup cans milk
1 tablespoon (15 ml) dried parsley flakes
¼ teaspoon garlic powder
455 g (16 ounces) cubed cheddar cheese
4 boneless, skinless chicken breast halves, cooked, diced

- Melt butter in large saucepan or roasting pan and sauté onion and carrots for 10 minutes, but do not brown. Add remaining ingredients and heat but do not boil.
- Reduce heat to low, cook until cheese melts and stir constantly. Serve piping hot. Serves 8.

TIP: This is really the 'easy' way to make chicken soup and if you are in an absolute rush, you could use leftover turkey or chicken.

Cheesy Chicken Soup

1 280-g (10-ounce) can cream of celery soup
1 280-g (10-ounce) can cream of chicken soup
½ soup can milk
½ cup shredded cheese
1 chicken breast, cooked, diced

- Mix all ingredients in saucepan on medium heat and stir until thoroughly hot. Serve hot. Serves 4 to 6.

Chicken-Rice Soup with Green Chillies

8 boneless, skinless chicken breast halves, cooked
1 litre carton chicken stock
1 cup (100 g) chopped celery
1 cup (185 g) rice
2–4 large fresh, green chillies, seeded, chopped

- Cut cooked chicken into small pieces and place in large saucepan.
- Add chicken stock, celery, rice, green chillies, 1 teaspoon salt and ¼ teaspoon pepper and simmer for about 35 minutes or until rice is tender. Serves 6.

Chicken and Rice Gumbo

1½ litres chicken stock
455 g (1 pound) boneless, skinless chicken breasts, cubed
2 425-g (15-ounce) cans corn kernels, drained
2 425-g (15-ounce) cans stewed tomatoes with liquid
¾ cup (140 g) white rice
1 teaspoon Cajun seasoning
1 cup okra, chopped

- Combine chicken stock and chicken in soup pot and cook on high heat for 15 minutes.
- Add remaining ingredients and 1 teaspoon pepper and bring to boil. Reduce heat and simmer for 30 minutes or until rice is done. Serves 8.

Creamy Chicken-Spinach Soup

255 g (9 ounces) refrigerated cheese-filled tortellini
1 litre carton chicken stock
1 280-g (10-ounce) can cream of chicken soup
2 chicken breast halves, cooked, chopped
280 g (10 ounces) frozen chopped spinach
2 cups (500 ml) milk
½ teaspoon dried thyme

- Cook pasta in soup pot with half chicken stock according to package directions.
- Stir in remaining stock, soup, chicken, ½ cup water, spinach, milk, 1 teaspoon salt, ½ teaspoon pepper and thyme.
- Bring to boil, reduce heat to low and simmer for 10 minutes. Serves 8.

Cold Night Bean Soup

1½ cups (395 g) cannellini beans
1½ litres chicken stock
4 tablespoons (55 g) butter
1 onion, chopped
1 clove garlic, minced
3 cups (420 g) chopped, cooked chicken
½ cup chopped green chillies
1½ teaspoons ground cumin
½ teaspoon cayenne pepper
Shredded Colby cheese

- Drain beans and add stock, butter, 1 cup (250 ml) water, onion and garlic. Bring to boil, reduce heat and cover. Simmer for 2 hours and stir occasionally. Add more water if needed.
- With potato masher, mash half beans. Add chicken, green chillies, cumin and cayenne pepper. Bring to boil, reduce heat and cover. Simmer for additional 30 minutes.
- When ready to serve, spoon in bowls and top with 1 to 2 tablespoons (10 to 15 g) cheese. Serves 8.

Quick Chicken-Pasta Soup

1 litre carton chicken stock
2 boneless, skinless chicken breast halves, cubed
1 230-g (8-ounce) can sliced carrots, drained
2 sticks celery, sliced
230 g (8 ounces) fettuccini (medium egg noodles) pasta

- Combine stock, chicken, carrots, celery and generous dash of pepper in large saucepan. Boil and cook for 3 minutes.
- Stir in pasta, reduce heat and cook for 10 minutes or until noodles are done; stir often. Serves 4 to 6.

Speedy Gonzalez Soup

2 cups chicken, cooked, diced
½ litre carton chicken stock
1 455-g (16-ounce) jar mild thick-and-chunky salsa
1 425-g (15-ounce) can baked beans

- Combine chicken, stock, salsa and beans in large saucepan.
- Bring to boil, reduce heat and simmer for 5 minutes. Serves 6.

TIP: If you have 1 (425 g/15 ounce) can corn kernels, add it for a crunchy texture.

Feel-Better Chicken-Noddle Soup

85 g (3 ounces) chicken-flavoured ramen noodles, broken
280 g (10 ounces) frozen green peas, thawed
2 teaspoons butter
1 115-g (4-ounce) jar sliced mushrooms, drained
3 cups (420 g) cooked, cubed chicken

- Heat 2¼ cups (560 ml) water in large saucepan to boiling.
- Add noodles, contents of seasoning packet, peas and butter. Heat to boiling, reduce heat to medium and cook for about 5 minutes.
- Stir in mushrooms and chicken and continue cooking over low heat until all ingredients heat through. To serve, spoon into serving bowls. Serves 6.

When reheating soup, use a double boiler. The hot water in the bottom part of the boiler does the trick with no burned or boiled-over soup.

Chicken-Veggie Surprise

1½ litres chicken stock
1 425-g (15-ounce) can sliced carrots, drained
1 425-g (15-ounce) can peas, drained
1 red capsicum, seeded, chopped
1 teaspoon dried tarragon
230 g (½ pound) boneless, skinless chicken breasts, cooked, cut into strips
455 g (16 ounces) frozen broccoli florets
115 g (4 ounces) linguine (thin egg noodles)

- Combine stock, carrots, peas, capsicum, tarragon and 1 teaspoon (5 ml) salt in large soup pot.
- Bring to boil, reduce heat and simmer for 5 minutes.
- Add chicken strips and broccoli and cook for an additional 10 minutes.
- Stir in noodles, bring to boil, reduce heat to medium and cook for 10 minutes or until noodles are tender. Serves 8.

Tempting Tortilla Soup

Don't let the number of ingredients keep you from serving this. It's really easy.

3 large boneless, skinless chicken breast halves, cooked, cubed
280 g (10 ounces) frozen corn, thawed
1 onion, chopped
1 litre carton chicken stock
2 280-g (10-ounce) cans tomatoes
2 chopped green chillies
2 teaspoons ground cumin
1 teaspoon chilli powder
1 clove garlic, minced
6 corn tortillas

- Combine all ingredients except tortillas in large soup pot. Bring to boil, reduce heat and simmer for 35 minutes.
- Preheat oven to 175° C (350° F).
- While soup simmers, cut tortillas into 2.5-cm (1-inch) strips and place on baking tray. Bake for about 5 minutes or until crisp. Serve tortilla strips with each serving of soup. Serves 6.

La Placita Enchilada Soup

6 boneless, skinless chicken breast halves
½ cup (115 g) butter
2 cloves garlic, minced
1 onion, minced
⅓ cup (40 g) flour
1 425-g (15-ounce) can stewed tomatoes, chopped
1 teaspoon paprika
3 chopped green chillies
480 g (1 pint) sour cream
230 g (8 ounces) shredded cheddar cheese

- Cook chicken with 12 cups (3 L) water in large saucepan until tender. Reserve broth, cube chicken and set aside. Melt butter in large roasting pan and cook garlic and onion until tender.
- Add 1 teaspoon salt to flour in bowl, slowly pour flour into butter mixture and stir constantly to dissolve all lumps.
- Continue stirring and slowly pour in reserved chicken broth. Cook until soup thickens to right consistency.
- Add chicken, tomatoes, green chillies and sour cream. Mix well and heat. Serve in individual bowls and sprinkle with cheese. Serves 6.

Screamin' Jalapeno Soup

3 carrots, peeled, diced
2 sticks celery, chopped
1 green capsicum, seeded, chopped
6 tablespoons (85 g) butter
1 litre carton chicken stock
3 cups (420 g) cooked, shredded chicken
3–5 jalapeno chillies, seeded, chopped
¼ cup (30 g) flour
1½ teaspoons ground cumin
500 ml (1 pint) carton pouring cream

- Combine carrots, celery and capsicum in large frypan and sauté in 4 tablespoons (55 g) butter.
- Transfer to large soup pot and add chicken stock, shredded chicken and chillies (3 for medium heat and 5 for serious heat). Bring to boil, reduce heat and simmer for about 30 minutes.
- In same frypan, melt remaining 2 tablespoons (30 g) butter and add flour and cumin.
- Heat mixture on medium-low heat, stirring constantly, to make a light brown roux.
- Stir in cream, stirring constantly, but do not boil.
- Pour cream mixture into vegetable-chicken mixture and heat on medium, stirring constantly, just until mixture thickens. Serves 6.

TIP: If you like it extra hot, leave the seeds and veins in the jalapenos. Wear rubber gloves when removing seeds from jalapenos.

Sopa de Lima

This is a traditional lime and tortilla soup.

4–6 boneless, skinless chicken breast halves
1 onion, minced
1 red capsicum, seeded, chopped
2 cloves garlic, minced
2 tablespoons (30 ml) canola oil
6 limes, divided
3 fresh jalapeno chillies, seeded, minced
3 tomatoes, peeled, seeded, chopped
1 litre carton chicken stock
8 corn tortillas

- Cook chicken, chop into small pieces in frypan and set aside. Cook onion, capsicum and garlic in saucepan with hot oil until onion is translucent.
- Cut 1 lime in half, juice lime and place 2 rind shells into saucepan. Slice remaining limes and set aside.
- Add jalapeno chillies, tomatoes and stock, simmer for about 10 minutes and discard lime shells. Season chicken with a little salt and pepper and add to saucepan.
- Cut tortillas in half and slice into narrow strips. Heat oil in large frypan and cook tortilla strips until crispy. Drain on paper towel and place in warm oven until all strips cook.
- Taste soup for seasonings. Pour into individual soup bowls and place lime slice and tortilla strips on top. Serves 8.

TIP: Wear rubber gloves when removing seeds from jalapeno chillies.

Seaside Soup Cancun

1½ litres chicken stock
1 bunch fresh coriander, coarsely chopped
3 boneless, skinless chicken breast halves
1 ear fresh corn, cut into 6 rounds
1 tablespoon (15 ml) ground cumin
2 tablespoons (30 g) butter
2 onions, chopped
1 red capsicum, thinly sliced
1 clove garlic, minced
2 tomatoes, chopped
1 green capsicum, seeded
½ teaspoon sugar
4 corn tortillas
Olive oil
4 tablespoons (60 ml) lime juice
Sour cream

- Bring chicken stock to boil in large saucepan over high heat. Add coriander, chicken, corn and cumin. Cook until chicken and corn are done, for about 15 minutes.

- Melt butter in frypan and add onion, red capsicum, garlic and tomatoes. Cook, stirring frequently for about 10 minutes.

- Cut green capsicum into 6-mm (¼-inch) rounds and add to frypan. Add tomato mixture and sugar to chicken mixture. Cook for additional 10 minutes.

- Cut tortillas into thin strips, fry in frypan with oil until crispy and drain. Stir in lime juice and pour soup into serving bowls. Garnish with strips of fried tortillas and 1 heaped tablespoon (15 ml) sour cream. Serves 8.

Fast Fiesta Soup

1 425-g (15-ounce) can stewed tomatoes
1 teaspoon paprika
1 425-g (15-ounce) can corn kernels
1 425-g (15-ounce) can borlotti beans with liquid
1 litre carton chicken stock
1 280-g (10-ounce) can cream of celery soup
1 cup chicken breast, cooked, chopped

- Combine tomatoes, paprika, corn, beans, stock and soup in large soup pot, heat for 10 minutes over medium heat and mix well.
- Stir in chicken with liquid and heat until thoroughly hot. Serves 6.

Oriental Chicken-Pasta Soup

85 g (3 ounces) chicken-flavoured ramen noodles
1 roast chicken, boned, skinned, cubed
2 medium stalks bok choy with leaves, thinly sliced
1 230-g (8-ounce) can sliced carrots, drained
1 red capsicum, seeded, chopped

- Break apart noodles, place in 3 cups (750 ml) water and heat in soup pot. Stir in chicken, bok choy, carrots and capsicum.
- Bring to boil, reduce heat and simmer for 3 minutes; stir occasionally. Stir in flavour packet from noodles and serve immediately. Serves 8.

Zesty Chicken Stew

8 boneless, skinless chicken thighs
¼ cup (30 g) flour
3 tablespoons (45 ml) olive oil
¾ teaspoon dried oregano
¾ teaspoon dried basil
1 large onion, chopped
1 cup (250 ml) white cooking wine
½ litre carton chicken stock
3 medium new (red) potatoes, peeled, diced
1 425-g (15-ounce) can diced tomatoes, drained
1 230-g (8-ounce) can sliced carrots, drained
3 tablespoons (45 ml) chopped fresh coriander
Brown rice, cooked

- Lightly dredge chicken in flour and shake to remove excess.
- Brown chicken in hot oil in large heavy pan over medium-high heat for 4 minutes on each side and set aside.
- Combine oregano, basil and a little salt and pepper in bowl and sprinkle mixture evenly over chicken.
- Sauté onion in remaining oil in large pan, stir in wine and cook for 2 minutes.
- Return chicken to pan and add stock, potatoes, tomatoes and carrots.
- Reduce heat and simmer, stirring occasionally for 45 minutes.
- Stir in coriander and serve over rice. Serves 8.

Wake-Up Chicken-Rice Stew

2 cups chicken, cooked, chopped
1 litre carton chicken stock
1 425-g (15-ounce) can stewed tomatoes
½ cup (130 g) hot salsa
2 cups (370 g) instant brown rice
1 425-g (15-ounce) can corn kernels
1 425-g (15-ounce) can cut green beans
½ teaspoon ground cumin
½ teaspoon chilli powder

- Combine chicken, stock, stewed tomatoes, salsa and rice in heavy soup pot.
- Bring to boil, reduce heat and simmer for 10 minutes.
- Stir in corn, green beans, cumin, chilli powder and a little salt and pepper.
- Bring to boil, reduce heat and cook for 5 minutes. Serves 6 to 8.

Favourite Chicken-Tomato Stew

455 g (1 pound) boneless, skinless chicken breast halves, cut into strips
1 onion, chopped
1 green capsicum, seeded, chopped
1 litre carton chicken stock
2 425-g (15-ounce) cans stewed tomatoes
2 teaspoons paprika
2 425-g (15-ounce) cans cannellini beans with liquid
1 cup (265 g) salsa
2 teaspoons ground cumin
1½ cups (85 g) crushed corn chips

- Brown and cook chicken in stew pot on medium heat for 10 minutes.
- Add onion, capsicum, stock, tomatoes, paprika, cannellini beans, salsa, cumin and a little salt and pepper.
- Bring to boil, reduce heat and simmer for 25 minutes, stirring often.
- Ladle into individual soup bowls and sprinkle crushed corn chips on top of stew. Serve immediately. Serves 8.

Sister's Brunswick Stew

This dish takes longer than most dishes, but it is so worth it. Cook meat one day and put stew together the next day. You'll have enough to freeze and serve for several meals. It makes an excellent one-dish meal.

910 g (2 pound) boneless pork loin
1.4 kg (3 pounds) boneless, skinless chicken pieces
4 medium potatoes, quartered
3 795-g (28-ounce) cans stewed, diced tomatoes
2 teaspoons sugar
1 medium onion, chopped
2 455-g (16-ounce) cans butter beans, drained
2 455-g (16-ounce) packets frozen corn, thawed

- Cut pork and chicken into bite-size pieces. Cover with water and cook in stew pot for 1 hour, very slowly or until tender. Skim off excess fat.
- Return meat to broth, add potatoes and cook on medium. When done, mash potatoes to thicken broth. Add tomatoes, sugar, a little salt and pepper and cook until soupy.
- Add onion and butter beans. Cook for 10 minutes on low and stir frequently.
- Add corn and cook for 5 minutes. Keep scraping bottom of pan to prevent sticking. Serves 8 to 10.

Chicken-Sausage Stew

455 g (16 ounces) frozen stew vegetables
2 cups chicken breast, cooked, chopped
230 g (½ pound) Italian sausage, sliced
2 425-g (15-ounce) cans Italian stewed tomatoes
½ litre carton chicken stock
¼ teaspoon cayenne pepper
1 cup (165 g) cooked rice

- Combine all ingredients except rice and add a little salt in large heavy soup pot.
- Bring to boil, reduce heat and simmer for 25 minutes.
- Stir in cooked rice during last 5 minutes of cooking time. Serves 8.

Whipped Chicken Chowder

3 cups (420 g) cooked, cubed chicken
½ litre chicken stock
2 280-g (10-ounce) cans creamy potato soup
1 large onion, chopped
3 sticks celery, sliced diagonally
455 g (16 ounces) frozen corn, thawed
⅔ cup (150 ml) pouring cream

- Combine all ingredients except cream in large soup pot with ¾ cup (175 ml) water.
- Cover and cook on low heat for about 45 minutes. Add cream and heat for additional 10 minutes on low. Do not boil. Serves 6.

Chicken-Broccoli Chowder

1 litre carton chicken stock
1 bunch fresh spring onions, finely chopped
280 g (10 ounces) frozen chopped broccoli florets
1½ cups (90 g) dry mashed potato flakes
2½ cups (350 g) cooked, cut-up chicken breasts
230 g (8 ounces) shredded mozzarella cheese
250 ml (8 ounces) pouring cream
1 cup (250 ml) milk

- Combine stock, half spring onions and broccoli in large saucepan. Bring to boil, reduce heat, cover and simmer for 5 minutes.
- Stir in dry potato flakes and mix until they blend well.
- Add chicken, cheese, cream, milk, 1 cup (250 ml) water and a little salt and pepper.
- Heat over medium heat and stir occasionally until hot and cheese melts, for about 5 minutes.
- Ladle into individual soup bowls and garnish with remaining chopped spring onions. Serves 8.

Rich Cheddar Chowder

1 litre carton chicken stock
4 baking potatoes, peeled, diced
1 onion, chopped
1 cup (110 g) shredded carrots
1 green and 1 red capsicum, seeded, chopped
¼ cup (60 g) butter
⅓ cup (40 g) flour
500 ml (1 pint) unthickened cream
1½ cups (375 g) milk
455 g (16 ounces) shredded sharp cheddar cheese
⅛–¼ teaspoon hot sauce

- Combine stock, potatoes, onion, carrots and capsicums in large soup pot. Bring to a boil, reduce heat and simmer for 15 minutes.
- Melt butter in large saucepan, add flour and stir until smooth. Cook for 1 minute and stir constantly. Gradually add cream and milk; cook over medium heat and stir constantly until mixture thickens.
- Add cheese and hot sauce to vegetable mixture and cook just until thoroughly hot; do not boil. Serves 6 to 8.

Mama Mia Chicken Chowder

2 cups chicken breast meat, cooked, chopped
¼ cup (60 ml) Italian salad dressing
1 425-g (15-ounce) can stewed tomatoes
1½ cups (375 ml) chicken stock
2 small zucchini, chopped
½ cup (55 g) elbow macaroni
1 teaspoon dried basil
1 cup (115 g) shredded mozzarella cheese

- Combine chicken, salad dressing, tomatoes, stock, zucchini, pasta, basil, ½ cup (125 ml) water and a little salt and pepper in large soup pot.
- Bring to boil, reduce heat and simmer for 10 minutes or until pasta is tender.
- Serve in individual soup bowls and sprinkle cheese over each serving. Serves 4 to 6.

If you have any leftover cooked pasta, meat or vegetables, use them for instant soup ingredients. Most cooked vegetables can also be pureed and stirred in to thicken soups.

Great Northern Chilli

2 onions, coarsely chopped
Olive oil
3 425-g (15-ounce) cans cannellini beans, drained
1 litre carton chicken stock
2 tablespoons (15 g) minced garlic
2 chopped green chillies
1 tablespoon (15 ml) ground cumin
3 cups (420 g) cooked, finely chopped chicken breasts
230 g (8 ounces) shredded Colby cheese

- Cook onions in a little oil in large, heavy pot for about 5 minutes, but do not brown.
- Place 1 can beans in shallow bowl and mash with fork.
- Add mashed beans, 2 remaining cans of beans, chicken stock, garlic, green chillies and cumin to soup pot. Bring to boil, reduce heat, cover and simmer for 30 minutes.
- Add chopped chicken, stir to blend well and heat until chilli is thoroughly hot.
- When serving, top each bowl with 3 tablespoons (20 g) cheese. Serves 6 to 8.

White Lightning Chilli

1½ cups (395 g) cannellini beans
1½ litres chicken stock
2 tablespoons (30 g) butter
1 onion, chopped
1 clove garlic, minced
3 cups (420 g) cooked, chopped chicken
1½ teaspoons ground cumin
½ teaspoon cayenne pepper
6 20-cm (8-inch) flour tortillas
Shredded Colby cheese

- Drain beans and place in soup pot and add stock, butter, onion and garlic.
- Bring to boil, reduce heat and cover. Simmer for 2 hours and stir occasionally.
- With potato masher, mash half of beans in soup pot. Add chicken, cumin and cayenne pepper. Bring to boil, reduce heat and cover. Simmer for additional 30 minutes.
- With kitchen shears, make 4 cuts in each tortilla towards centre, but not completely through centre. Line serving bowls with tortillas and overlap cut edges.
- Spoon in chilli and top with cheese. Serves 6 to 8.

Guess-What Chilli

1 onion, chopped
1 red capsicum, chopped
1 green capsicum, chopped
Olive oil
2 tablespoons (15 g) minced garlic
2 tablespoons (15 g) chilli powder
3 teaspoons ground cumin
910 g (2 pounds) boneless, skinless chicken breast halves, cooked, cubed
1 litre carton chicken stock
3 425-g (15-ounce) cans borlotti beans

- Cook onions and capsicums in large, heavy soup pot over medium heat with a little oil for about 5 minutes and stir occasionally.
- Add garlic, chilli powder, cumin and cubed chicken and cook for additional 10 minutes.
- Stir in stock and a little salt. Bring to boil, reduce heat, cover and simmer for 15 minutes.
- Place 1 can beans in shallow bowl and mash with fork. Add mashed beans and remaining 2 cans beans to pot.
- Bring to boil, reduce heat and simmer for 10 minutes. Serves 8.

TIP: *This is delicious served with hot, buttered flour tortillas or spooned over small, original corn chips for a great one-dish meal.*

Make-Believe Chilli Supper

455 g (1 pound) boneless, skinless chicken breast halves, cubed
¼ cup (60 g) butter
3 sticks celery, sliced
2 onions, chopped
1 red capsicum, seeded, chopped
2 teaspoons minced garlic
3 425-g (15-ounce) cans cannellini beans with liquid
1 litre carton chicken stock
2 teaspoons ground cumin
1 teaspoon dried oregano
2 chopped green chillies
1 230-g (8-ounce) carton sour cream

- Preheat oven to 175° C (350° F).
- Sprinkle 1 teaspoon (5 ml) salt on chicken and place in sprayed 23 x 33-cm (9 x 13-inch) baking dish and bake for 15 minutes.
- Melt butter in soup pot and cook celery, onions, capsicum and garlic on medium heat for 10 to 15 minutes.
- Stir in cooked chicken, beans, stock, cumin, oregano and green chillies and mix well.
- Bring to boil, reduce heat and simmer for 15 minutes. Stir in sour cream. Serves 8.

White Bean Chilli

455 g (1 pound) cannellini beans
2 onions, finely chopped
2 sticks celery, sliced
2 tablespoons (30 ml) olive oil
2 chopped green chillies
2 tablespoons (15 g) minced garlic
1 tablespoon (5 g) ground cumin
2 teaspoons dried oregano
½ teaspoon cayenne pepper
1½ litres chicken stock
1 roast chicken, boned, cubed
340 g (12 ounces) shredded Colby cheese

- Drain beans and set aside.
- Sauté onions and celery in hot oil in saucepan.
- Add green chillies, garlic, cumin, oregano and cayenne pepper, cook for 2 minutes and stir constantly.
- Transfer to soup pot and add beans, chicken stock and ½ cup (125 ml) water.
- Bring to boil and reduce heat. Cover, simmer for about 2 hours or until beans are tender; stir occasionally.
- Add chicken and 1 cup (115 g) cheese. Bring to boil, reduce heat and simmer for 10 minutes, stirring often.
- Ladle chilli into individual soup bowls and top each serving with remaining cheese. Serves 8.

Cheesy Tomato Chilli

1 795-g (28-ounce) can diced tomatoes
1 425-g (15-ounce) can kidney beans, rinsed, drained
1 425-g (15-ounce) can borlotti beans, drained
1 litre carton chicken stock
2 cups cooked chicken breasts, chopped
1 tablespoon (15 ml) chilli powder
230 g (8 ounces) shredded cheddar cheese

- Combine tomatoes, kidney beans, borlotti beans, stock, chicken, chilli powder and a little salt and pepper in soup pot.
- Bring to boil, reduce heat and simmer for 25 minutes.
- Stir in half cheese and spoon into individual soup bowls.
- Sprinkle remaining cheese on top of each serving. Serves 8.

Corny Turkey Soup

¼ cup (60 g) butter
1 small onion, chopped
1 red capsicum, seeded, chopped
85 g (3 ounces) cream cheese, cubed
1 425-g (15-ounce) can creamed corn
1 425-g (15-ounce) can corn kernels
½ litre carton chicken stock
½ cup (125 ml) milk
2 cups (280 g) cooked, cubed turkey
4 fresh spring onions, sliced

- Melt butter in large, heavy soup pot, cook onion and capsicum and stir often. Add cream cheese and creamed corn and cook on medium heat, stir constantly until cheese melts.
- Add corn kernels, stock, milk and turkey, mix well and cook until soup is thoroughly hot. Sprinkle sliced spring onions over top of each serving. Serves 4 to 6.

A pinch of dried chilli flakes makes a wonderful addition to most soups.

Creamy Turkey Soup

1½ litres chicken stock
455 g (1 pound) pontiac potatoes, peeled, cubed
3 sticks celery, sliced
1 425-g (15-ounce) can sliced carrots, drained
1 cup chopped yellow squash
2 teaspoons minced garlic
1 teaspoon dried thyme
1½ cups (210 g) cooked, shredded turkey
1 280-g (10-ounce) can cream of chicken soup
1 cup (250 ml) milk or unthickened cream

- Combine chicken stock, potatoes and celery in soup pot and boil. Add a little salt and pepper and cook on medium heat for about 20 minutes or until potatoes and celery are tender. Add carrots, squash, garlic and thyme and cook for additional 10 minutes.
- Stir in shredded turkey, chicken soup and milk and heat just until soup is thoroughly hot, but do not boil. Serves 8.

Turkey with Avocado Soup

3 large potatoes, peeled, cubed
1 litre carton chicken stock
1 teaspoon ground thyme
230 g (½ pound) smoked turkey breast, cubed
280 g (10 ounces) frozen corn
3 slices bacon, cooked crisp, drained
1 large avocado
4 roma tomatoes, coarsely chopped
1 lime

- Combine potatoes, stock and thyme in soup pot, cover and bring to boil. Reduce heat and simmer until potatoes are tender, for about 15 minutes.
- With slotted spoon transfer half of potatoes to blender or food processor, puree and pour into soup pot.
- Add turkey, remaining potatoes and corn and simmer for 5 minutes.
- Crumble bacon; peel and slice avocado.
- Add bacon, avocado, tomatoes, juice of lime and a little salt and pepper to turkey mixture. Stir gently to mix. Serves 8.

TIP: Peel and cut avocado just before serving, because they turn dark so quickly.

Last-Minute Turkey Help

1 litre carton chicken stock
1 small zucchini, sliced
455 g (16 ounces) frozen vegetable mix
1½ cups (210 g) cooked, cubed turkey
4 fresh spring onions, sliced

- Combine stock, ¼ cup (60 ml) water, zucchini, vegetable mix and cubed turkey in large saucepan.
- Bring to boil, reduce heat and simmer for 10 to 12 minutes or until vegetables are tender.
- Garnish each serving with sliced spring onions before serving. Serves 6.

So Easy, Creamy Turkey Soup

1 280-g (10-ounce) can cream of celery soup
1 280-g (10-ounce) can cream of chicken soup
1 soup can filled with milk
1 cup (140 g) finely diced turkey

- Combine all ingredients in large saucepan. Serve hot. Serves 4.

Tasty Turkey-Veggie Soup

1 litre carton chicken stock
2 teaspoons minced garlic
455 g (16 ounces) frozen corn
280 g (10 ounces) frozen cut green beans
280 g (10 ounces) frozen sliced carrots
2 425-g (15-ounce) cans stewed tomatoes
2½ cups (350 g) cooked, cubed turkey
1 cup (115 g) shredded mozzarella cheese

- Combine stock, garlic, corn, green beans, carrots, tomatoes, turkey and 1 teaspoon (5 ml) salt in large, heavy soup pot.
- Bring to boil, reduce heat and simmer for 15 minutes.
- Before serving, top each bowl of soup with mozzarella cheese. Serves 8.

Hearty 15-Minute Turkey Soup

This is great served with cornbread.

½ litre carton chicken stock
3 425-g (15-ounce) cans cannellini beans with liquid
1 795-g (28-ounce) can stewed tomatoes with liquid
3 cups (420 g) cooked, cubed white turkey
2 teaspoons minced garlic
¼ teaspoon cayenne pepper
170 g (6 ounces) baby spinach, stems removed

- Combine stock, beans, stewed tomatoes, turkey, garlic, cayenne pepper and a little salt and pepper in soup pot.
- Bring to boil, reduce heat and simmer on medium heat for about 10 minutes.
- Stir in baby spinach, bring to boil and cook, stirring constantly, for 5 minutes. Serves 8.

Turkey Tango

This is spicy, but not too spicy. It's just right! Try it with chicken too.

3–4 cups (420–560 g) chopped turkey
1 litre carton chicken stock
2 280-g (10-ounce) cans diced tomatoes
2 chopped green chillies
1 425-g (15-ounce) can corn kernels, drained
1 large onion, chopped
1 280-g (10-ounce) can tomato soup
1 teaspoon garlic powder
1 teaspoon dried oregano
3 tablespoons (25 g) cornflour

- Combine turkey, stock, tomatoes, green chillies, corn, onion, tomato soup, garlic powder and oregano in large roasting pan.
- Mix cornflour with 3 tablespoons (45 ml) water and add to soup mixture.
- Bring mixture to a boil, reduce heat and simmer for 2 hours. Stir occasionally. Serves 6 to 8.

Smoked Turkey-Sausage Soup

2 tablespoons (30 ml) olive oil
1 small onion, chopped
1 green capsicum, seeded, chopped
½ litre carton chicken stock
1 medium potato, peeled, cubed
½ teaspoon dried basil
455 g (1 pound) smoked turkey Polish sausage, sliced
1 425-g (15-ounce) can cannellini beans with liquid

- Combine oil, onion and capsicum in soup pot and cook for 5 minutes. Stir in stock, potato, basil, turkey sausage and a little salt and pepper. Bring to boil, reduce heat to medium and simmer for 15 minutes or until potato is tender.

- Stir in beans and heat just until soup is thoroughly hot. Serves 6.

Fast Gobbler Fix

1 onion, chopped
1 red capsicum, chopped
1 green capsicum, chopped
Olive oil
2 85-g (3-ounce) packets chicken-flavoured ramen noodles
2 280-g (10-ounce) cans cream of chicken soup
1 cup (140 g) cooked, cubed turkey

- Cook onions and capsicums in soup pot with a little oil just until tender but not brown. Add noodles with seasoning packet and 4 cups (1 L) water. Cook for 5 minutes or until noodles are tender.

- Stir in chicken soup and cubed turkey. Heat, stirring constantly, until thoroughly hot. Serves 6.

Turkey and Rice Soup

¼ cup (60 g) butter
1 onion, chopped
3 sticks celery, finely chopped
1 capsicum, seeded, chopped
1 litre carton chicken stock
1 170-g (6-ounce) box long grain-wild rice
2 280-g (10-ounce) cans cream of chicken soup
2 cups (480 ml) cooked, diced white meat turkey
1 cup (250 ml) milk

- Melt butter in soup pot over medium heat. Add onion, celery and capsicum and cook for 10 minutes.
- Add chicken stock and rice and bring to boil. Reduce heat and cook on low for about 15 minutes or until rice is tender.
- Stir in chicken soup, turkey, milk and ¾ teaspoon pepper. Stir constantly and cook on medium heat until mixture is thoroughly hot. Serves 6.

Turkey Tenders Gobble

½ cup (95 g) wild rice
3 sticks celery, sliced
1 onion, chopped
1 115-g (4-ounce) can sliced mushrooms, drained
¼ cup (60 g) butter
1 litre carton chicken stock
680 g (1½ pounds) turkey tenderloins
1 425-g (15-ounce) can stewed tomatoes

- Mix all ingredients in soup pot and bring to boil. Reduce heat and simmer for 45 to 55 minutes or until wild rice is tender.
- Remove turkey tenderloins with slotted spoon, cut into bite-size pieces and add to soup mixture. Heat just until thoroughly hot and serve. Serves 6.

Cajun Turkey Gumbo

1 litre carton chicken stock
455 g (1 pound) cooked turkey, cubed
1 425-g (15-ounce) can corn kernels
2 425-g (15-ounce) cans stewed tomatoes
1 cup chopped okra
¾ cup (70 g) instant rice
2 teaspoons minced garlic
1 teaspoon Cajun seasoning

- Combine all ingredients in large soup pot and bring to boil. Reduce heat and simmer for 15 minutes. Serves 8.

Turkey-Chilli Dinner

1 onion, finely chopped
2 425-g (15-ounce) cans cannellini beans
1 litre carton chicken stock
2 diced green chillies
2 teaspoons ground cumin
1 teaspoon dried oregano
¼ teaspoon cayenne pepper
4 cups (450 g) cooked, cubed turkey
340 g (12 ounces) shredded Colby cheese

- Combine all ingredients except cheese in soup pot and boil. Reduce heat and simmer for 20 minutes.
- Just before serving, stir in about 2 cups (230 g) cheese and stir constantly. Ladle into individual soup bowls and sprinkle remaining cheese on top. Serves 6.

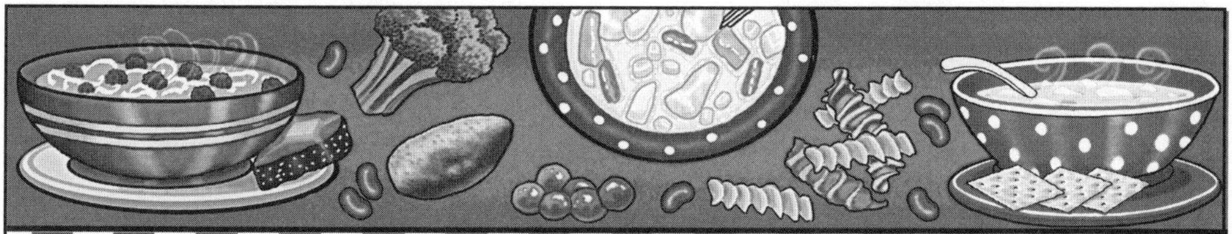

Big Bold Beefy Bowls

These beefy soups, stews and chillies are sure to please.

Big Bold Beefy Bowls Contents

Fresh Beefy Vegetable Soup

455 g (1 pound) lean minced beef
1 onion, chopped
1 425-g (15-ounce) can Italian stewed tomatoes
1 cup (165 g) freshly cut corn
1 large potato, peeled, cubed
3 sticks celery, sliced
1 carrot, thinly sliced
1 230-g (8-ounce) can green peas or lima beans
1 teaspoon dried Italian seasoning
½ teaspoon hot sauce
1 litre carton beef stock
2 tablespoons flour

- Brown beef and onion in large, heavy soup pot over medium heat.
- Add stewed tomatoes, corn, potato, celery, carrot, peas, Italian seasoning, hot sauce, beef stock and 1 cup (250 ml) water. Bring to boil, reduce heat and simmer for 1 hour.
- Combine flour and ¼ cup (60 ml) water in bowl and stir to make paste.
- On medium heat, add paste to soup with a little salt and pepper and cook, stirring constantly until soup thickens. Serves 6 to 8.

Speedy Vegetable Soup

455 g (1 pound) lean minced beef
2 425-g (15-ounce) cans stewed tomatoes
1½ litres beef stock
455 g (16 ounces) frozen mixed vegetables
½ cup (95 g) instant brown rice

- Brown beef in frypan, cook and stir until beef crumbles.
- Transfer to soup pot and add tomatoes, beef stock and vegetables.
- Bring to boil, reduce heat and simmer for 20 minutes, stirring occasionally.
- Add brown rice and cook on medium heat for 5 minutes. Serves 8.

Beefy Veggie Soup

455 g (1 pound) lean minced beef
1 1.4-L (46-ounce) can mixed vegetable juice
30 g (1 ounce) onion soup mix
85 g (3 ounces) beef-flavoured ramen noodles
455 g (16 ounces) frozen mixed vegetables

- Cook beef until no longer pink in large soup pot over medium heat. Drain. Stir in vegetable juice, soup mix, seasoning packet in noodles and mixed vegetables.
- Heat mixture to boiling, reduce heat and simmer for 6 minutes or until vegetables are tender but crisp. Bring to boil again, stir in noodles and cook for 3 minutes. Serves 8.

Franks and Veggie Soup

¼ cup (60 g) butter
2 onions, finely chopped
1 red capsicum, seeded, chopped
2 teaspoons minced garlic
1 795-g (28-ounce) can baked beans
280 g (10 ounces) frozen mixed vegetables
½ litre carton beef stock
6 frankfurters, cut into 2.5-cm (1-inch) slices
1 tablespoon (15 ml) Worcestershire sauce
1 cup (115 g) shredded Colby cheese

- Melt butter in large saucepan over medium heat and cook onions, capsicum and garlic for 5 minutes.
- Stir in beans, mixed vegetables, stock, frankfurters and Worcestershire. Cook over medium heat for 5 minutes and stir occasionally.
- Ladle into individual soup bowls and sprinkle each serving with cheese. Serves 8.

Mother's Beef-Veggie Soup

455 g (1 pound) lean minced beef
30 g (1 ounce) onion soup mix
1 litre carton beef stock
2 425-g (15-ounce) cans stewed tomatoes
2 425-g (15-ounce) cans mixed vegetables with liquid
1 cup (105 g) shell pasta

- Brown beef in soup pot over high heat and drain. Reduce heat to medium and add soup mix, stock, tomatoes and mixed vegetables and cook for 5 minutes.
- Stir in pasta and cook on medium-high heat for 15 minutes or until pasta is tender, stirring occasionally. Serves 8.

Vegetable-Beef Soup

680 g (1½ pounds) lean minced beef
3 425-g (15-ounce) cans mixed vegetables with liquid
30 g (1 ounce) onion soup mix
1 1.4-L (48-ounce) can mixed vegetable juice
½ litre carton beef stock
½ cup (100 g) barley

- Brown beef in roasting pan, stir to crumble and drain.
- Add all remaining ingredients, bring to boil and simmer for 15 minutes. Serves 8.

Country-Style Beefy Soup

680 g (1½ pounds) lean minced beef
1 onion, chopped
1 red capsicum, chopped
1 green capsicum, chopped
2 teaspoons minced garlic
1 litre carton beef stock
2 425-g (15-ounce) cans Italian stewed tomatoes
3 teaspoons Italian seasoning
1½ cups (160 g) macaroni
Shredded cheddar cheese

- Brown and cook beef, onions, capsicums and garlic in soup pot on medium heat. Add beef stock, stewed tomatoes and Italian seasoning and boil for 2 minutes.
- Add pasta and cook, stirring occasionally on medium heat for about 15 minutes. When serving, sprinkle cheese over each serving. Serves 6 to 8.

In France in the 16th century, soup was called 'restaurer' and was sold by street vendors. It was believed to be a remedy for exertion – a restorative. In 1765, a shop was opened in Paris to sell 'restaurers' and we now call stores selling prepared meals restaurants.

Italian Vegetable Soup

455 g (1 pound) lean minced beef
2 teaspoons minced garlic
1 green capsicum, seeded, chopped
1 litre carton beef stock
1 425-g (15-ounce) can Italian stewed tomatoes
2 small zucchini, sliced
1 425-g (15-ounce) can cannellini beans, rinsed, drained
280 g (10 ounces) frozen chopped spinach, thawed

- Brown and cook beef and garlic in soup pot for 5 minutes or until beef crumbles.
- Stir in capsicum, stock, tomatoes, zucchini and beans and cook on medium heat for 15 minutes.
- Add spinach and continue cooking for additional 10 minutes. Serves 6.

Italian Beefy Veggie Soup

455 g (1 pound) lean minced beef
2 teaspoons minced garlic
2 425-g (15-ounce) cans Italian stewed tomatoes
1 litre carton beef stock
2 teaspoons Italian seasoning
455 g (16 ounces) frozen mixed vegetables
⅓ cup (35 g) shell pasta
230 g (8 ounces) shredded Cheddar cheese

- Cook beef and garlic in large soup pot for 5 minutes.
- Stir in tomatoes, stock, seasoning, mixed vegetables, pasta and a little salt and pepper.
- Bring to boil, reduce heat and simmer for 10 to 15 minutes or until pasta is tender.
- Ladle into individual serving bowls and sprinkle several tablespoons cheese over top of soup. Serves 8.

Almost all soups can be made in advance. Many, in fact, are better on the second or third day, after the flavours have blended.

No-Brainer Heidelberg Soup

2 280-g (10-ounce) cans potato soup
1 280-g (10-ounce) can cream of celery soup
1 soup can milk
6 slices salami, chopped
10 spring onions, chopped

- Cook potato soup, celery soup and milk in large saucepan on medium heat, stirring constantly, just until thoroughly hot.
- Sauté salami and onions in sprayed frypan and add to soup.
- Heat thoroughly and serve hot. Serves 6.

Easy Mexican Beef Soup

910 g (2 pounds) lean minced beef
2 425-g (15-ounce) jars chunky vegetable pasta sauce
1½ litres beef stock
2 425-g (15-ounce) cans stewed tomatoes
3 diced green chillies

- Brown beef until no longer pink in frypan and transfer to soup pot.
- Add pasta sauce, stock, stewed tomatoes, green chillies, 1 teaspoon (5 ml) salt and stir well.
- Cover and cook on medium-low heat for about 45 minutes. Serves 8.

Southwestern Soup

680 g (1½ pounds) lean minced beef
1 large onion, chopped
2 425-g (15-ounce) cans borlotti beans with liquid
1 425-g (15-ounce) can baked beans
2 425-g (15-ounce) cans corn kernels with liquid
2 425-g (15-ounce) cans stewed tomatoes
60 g (2 ounces) taco seasoning

- Brown beef and onion in large soup pot, stir until beef crumbles and drain.
- Add beans, corn, tomatoes and 1½ cups (375 ml) water.
- Bring to boil, reduce heat and stir in taco seasoning. Simmer for 25 minutes. Serves 8.

Kitchen-Sink Taco Soup

570 g (1¼ pounds) lean minced beef
1 onion, chopped
10 g (0.4 ounce) French onion soup mix
2 425-g (15-ounce) cans borlotti beans with liquid
1 425-g (15-ounce) can corn kernels with liquid
1 425-g (15-ounce) can creamed corn
3 425-g (15-ounce) cans stewed tomatoes with liquid
3 teaspoons paprika
Corn chips
230 g (8 ounces) shredded Colby cheese

- Brown minced beef and onion in frypan, drain and stir in soup mix.
- Combine beef-onion mixture, beans, corn, creamed corn, stewed tomatoes and paprika in roasting pan.
- Bring to boil, lower heat and simmer for 10 to 15 minutes.
- Serve over corn chips and sprinkle with cheese. Serves 6.

Cantina Taco Soup

680 g (1½ pounds) lean minced beef
30 g (1 ounce) taco seasoning
2 425-g (15-ounce) cans stewed tomatoes
2 teaspoons paprika
1 425-g (15-ounce) can corn kernels, drained
Crushed corn chips
Shredded cheddar cheese

- Brown beef in frypan until it is no longer pink and transfer to soup pot.
- Add taco seasoning, tomatoes, corn and 1 cup (250 ml) water.
- On high heat, bring to boil, reduce heat and simmer for about 35 minutes.
- When serving, spoon 1 heaped tablespoon (15 ml) crushed corn chips and 1 heaped tablespoon (10 g) cheese over each serving. Serves 4 to 6.

If your soup is not intended as the main course, you can count on one quart (litre) to serve six people. As a main dish, plan on two servings per quart (litre).

Across-the-Border Soup

455 g (1 pound) lean minced beef
1 onion, chopped
1 red capsicum, chopped
1 green capsicum, chopped
2 tablespoons (30 ml) olive oil
280 g (10 ounces) frozen corn
1 litre carton beef stock
1 425-g (15-ounce) can borlotti beans with liquid
2 tablespoons (30 ml) chilli powder
1 teaspoon ground cumin
1 795-g (28-ounce) jar pasta sauce with meatballs

- Brown beef, onions and capsicums in oil in large frypan.
- Transfer to soup pot and add corn, stock, beans, chilli powder, cumin and a little salt and pepper.
- Bring to boil, reduce heat and simmer for 30 minutes. About 15 minutes prior to serving, add meatballs and sauce and heat thoroughly. Serve hot. Serves 8.

Albondigas Soup

This is a very traditional meatball-potato soup.

910 g (2 pounds) lean minced beef
1 cup (60 g) breadcrumbs
1 onion, chopped
2 eggs
2 teaspoons ground cumin
2 cloves garlic, minced
¼ cup (55 g) butter
2 tablespoons (15 g) flour
3 tablespoons (20 g) snipped coriander
2 large potatoes, peeled, cubed

- Combine beef, breadcrumbs, onion, eggs, cumin and garlic with 1 teaspoon salt and ½ teaspoon pepper in bowl. Mix well and form into meatballs about 2.5 cm (1¼ inches) in diameter.
- Brown meatballs on all sides in large frypan. Transfer to bowl and set aside.
- Heat butter in same frypan and sprinkle flour on top. Stir constantly until flour browns. (Do not burn.)
- Add 4 cups (1 L) hot water, coriander and ½ teaspoon salt and continue to stir until liquid boils.
- Add potatoes and meatballs and simmer until potatoes are done. Serves 6.

Quick Enchilada Soup

455 g (1 pound) lean minced beef, browned, drained
1 425-g (15-ounce) can stewed tomatoes
2 425-g (15-ounce) cans borlotti beans with liquid
1 425-g (15-ounce) can corn kernels with liquid
1 onion, chopped
2 280-g (10-ounce) cans enchilada sauce
230 g (8 ounces) shredded cheese

- Combine beef, tomatoes, beans, corn, onion, enchilada sauce and 1 cup (250 ml) water in soup pot.
- Bring to boil, reduce heat and simmer for 35 minutes.
- When serving, sprinkle a little shredded cheese over each serving. Serves 6.

Easy Meaty Minestrone

2 740-g (26-ounce) cans minestrone soup
1 425-g (15-ounce) can borlotti beans with liquid
510 g (18 ounces) frozen meatballs, thawed
145 g (5 ounces) grated parmesan cheese

- Combine soups, beans, meatballs and ½ cup (125 ml) water in large saucepan.
- Bring to boil, reduce heat and simmer for about 15 minutes.
- To serve, sprinkle each serving with parmesan cheese. Serves 6.

Spaghetti Soup

200 g (7 ounces) spaghetti, broken
510 g (18 ounces) frozen, cooked meatballs, thawed
1 795-g (28-ounce) jar spaghetti sauce
1 425-g (15-ounce) can stewed tomatoes

- Cook spaghetti in soup pot with 2 quarts (2 L) boiling water and a little salt for about 6 minutes (no need to drain).
- When spaghetti is done, add meatballs, spaghetti sauce and stewed tomatoes and cook until mixture heats through. Serves 8.

TIP: If you want to garnish each soup bowl, sprinkle with 2 tablespoons (15 g) shredded mozzarella cheese or whatever cheese you have in the refrigerator.

Quick Beef-Veggie Soup

455 g (1 pound) round steak, cubed
1 litre carton beef stock
1 170-g (6-ounce) can tomato soup
1 425-g (15-ounce) can stewed tomatoes
1 teaspoon paprika
1 425-g (15-ounce) can mixed vegetables with liquid
1 230-g (8-ounce) can corn kernels, drained

- Brown steak on medium heat in soup pot for 10 minutes. Add beef stock and tomato soup and simmer for 15 minutes.
- Stir in stewed tomatoes, paprika, mixed vegetables and corn and cook for additional 10 minutes. Serves 6.

Chunky Beefy Pasta Soup

455 g (1 pound) beef round steak, cubed
1 onion, chopped
2 sticks celery, sliced
1 tablespoon (15 ml) oil
1 tablespoon (15 ml) chilli powder
½ teaspoon dried oregano
1 425-g (15-ounce) can stewed tomatoes
1 litre carton beef stock
½ 230-g (8-ounce) package fettuccini (egg noodles) pasta
1 green capsicum, seeded, chopped

- Cook and stir cubed steak, onion and celery in soup pot with oil for 15 minutes or until beef browns.
- Stir in 1 cup (250 ml) water, 1 teaspoon salt, chilli powder, oregano, stewed tomatoes and beef stock.
- Bring to boil, reduce heat and simmer for 1 hour 30 minutes to 2 hours or until beef is tender.
- Stir in pasta and capsicum and heat to boiling.
- Reduce heat and simmer for 10 to 15 minutes or until pasta is tender. Serves 6.

Meatball Soup

510 g (18 ounces) frozen, cooked meatballs
1 litre carton beef stock
2 425-g (15-ounce) cans Italian stewed tomatoes
455 g (16 ounces) frozen stew vegetables

- Place meatballs, beef stock and stewed tomatoes in large saucepan.
- Bring to boil, reduce heat and simmer for 10 minutes or until meatballs are thoroughly hot.
- Add vegetables and cook on medium heat for 10 minutes. Serves 6 to 8.

TIP: If you like your soup thicker, mix 2 tablespoons (15 g) cornflour in ¼ cup (60 ml) water and stir into soup, bring to boiling and stir constantly until soup thickens.

Steak Soup

455 g (1 pound) ground sirloin steak
2 280-g (10-ounce) cans vegetable soup
2 280-g (10-ounce) cans tomatoes
2 chopped green chillies

- Brown ground sirloin in large frypan, crumble and drain.
- Stir in soups, tomatoes and green chillies.
- Heat on medium-low for 15 to 20 minutes or until hot. Stir often. Serves 4.

Black Bean-Barbecue Soup

1 onion, finely chopped
2 tablespoons (30 ml) olive oil
2 teaspoons minced garlic
1 litre carton chicken stock
2 cups black beans, soaked, rinsed
1 280-g (10-ounce) can diced tomatoes
2 chopped green chillies
455 g (1 pound) shredded roast beef
2 tablespoons (30 ml) red wine vinegar
Shredded Colby cheese

- Sauté onion in oil in soup pot over medium heat, stir in garlic and sauté 1 more minute.
- Stir in stock, beans, tomatoes and green chillies. Reduce heat and simmer, stirring often for 15 minutes.
- Process 1 cup (250 ml) bean mixture in food processor until smooth.
- Return puree to soup pot, add beef and simmer for 10 minutes.
- Stir in vinegar and garnish each bowl with cheese. Serves 6 to 8.

Savoury soups and stews often taste better if made a day or two in advance and reheated just before serving.

Menudo

This could also be called Mexican Hangover Helper or at least it is reported to be a sure cure for the morning after.

910 g (2 pounds) tripe
1 bunch spring onions with tops, chopped
3 cloves garlic, minced
¾ cup (10 g) snipped fresh coriander leaves, divided
Fresh lime slices

- Wash tripe very well and dry with paper towels. Place tripe in soup pot with enough water to cover plus 8 cm (3 inches).
- Add onions and garlic, bring to boil, reduce heat and simmer for 6 to 8 hours until tripe is tender. Add water if necessary.
- When tripe is tender, remove from pot and cool for about 15 minutes. Cut into small pieces and return to soup pot.
- Add ¼ cup (5 g) coriander and cook for an additional 1 to 2 hours. Serve in large soup bowls and garnish with coriander and lime slices. Serves 4.

TIP: Menudo or tripe soup is a favourite in Mexico. Tripe is the inner lining of beef stomach, it's very tough and requires long cooking times.

Blue Norther Stew

Cold fronts in the south of America are called northers. This is a great choice for one of those cold, winter days.

680 g (1½ pounds) lean minced beef
1 onion, chopped
10 g (0.4 ounce) taco seasoning
10 g (0.4 ounce) French onion soup mix
1 425-g (15-ounce) can corn kernels, drained
1 425-g (15-ounce) can kidney beans with liquid
2 425-g (15-ounce) cans borlotti beans
2 425-g (15-ounce) cans stewed tomatoes
1 teaspoon paprika
1 280-g (10-ounce) can tomatoes
2 chopped green chillies

- Brown beef and onion in large roasting pan.
- Add both packets seasonings and mix well.
- Add corn, beans, stewed tomatoes, tomatoes, paprika, green chillies and 1 cup (250 ml) water, mix well and simmer for about 30 minutes. Serves 8.

Bronco Stew

Hang on for this hot ride!

910 g (2 pounds) minced round beef
Olive oil
1 onion, chopped
1 red capsicum, chopped
1 green capsicum, chopped
½ litre carton beef stock
30 g (1 ounce) taco seasoning
2 425-g (15-ounce) cans stewed tomatoes
2 teaspoons paprika
2 425-g (15-ounce) cans borlotti beans
455 g (16 ounces) cubed cheddar cheese
370 g (13 ounces) corn chips, crushed

- Brown beef on all sides in a little oil in stew pot on high heat and stir often.
- Add onion and capsicums, and cook for 3 minutes.
- Add stock and taco seasoning, reduce heat and simmer for 35 to 45 minutes or until most of liquid evaporates.
- Stir in tomatoes and beans and heat just until mixture is thoroughly hot. Add cheese and stir until cheese melts.
- Place about ¾ cup (40 g) crushed chips in bottom of individual soup bowls, spoon stew over chips and serve immediately. Serves 8.

Vegetable-Beef Stew

455 g (1 pound) stew meat
½ litre carton beef stock
1 795-g (28-ounce) can stewed tomatoes
2 425-g (15-ounce) cans mixed vegetables with liquid
½ cup (100 g) barley

- Combine meat, stock and 2 cups (250 ml) water and a little salt and pepper in large stew pot and bring to boil.
- Reduce heat to low and cook for 1 hour.
- Stir in all remaining ingredients and cook on medium heat for 30 minutes. Serves 6.

Minute Stew

455 g (1 pound) extra lean minced beef
½ litre carton beef stock
1 425-g (15-ounce) can stewed tomatoes
1 230-g (8-ounce) can corn kernels, drained
1 425-g (15-ounce) can mixed vegetables

- Brown ground meat in frypan and drain.
- Add stock, tomatoes, corn and vegetables to frypan and mix well.
- Simmer for 20 to 30 minutes and stir often. Serves 6.

Quick Brunswick Stew

Brunswick Stew is a favourite in Virginia and other southern U.S. states. The original version takes all day to make, but this is a quick substitute that is great in a pinch.

2 425-g (15-ounce) cans beef stew
1 425-g (15-ounce) can lima beans with liquid
2 425-g (15-ounce) cans stewed tomatoes with liquid
1 425-g (15-ounce) can corn kernels
½ teaspoon hot sauce

- Combine beef stew, beans, tomatoes and corn in large stew pot on medium heat. Bring to a boil, reduce heat and simmer for 20 minutes.
- Brunswick Stew needs to be a little spicy, so stir in ¼ teaspoon hot sauce at first, taste and add more if needed. If you don't want spicy, add 1 tablespoon (15 ml) Worcestershire sauce to stew. It is best served with hot cornbread. Serves 6.

Fresh chopped parsley added in the last few minutes of cooking adds a wonderful fresh flavour to soups and stews.

Baked Borlotti Bean Stew

1 cup (125 g) dried borlotti beans
455 g (1 pound) beef stew meat
1 onion, chopped
1 230-g (6-ounce) can tomato paste
¼ cup (55 g) brown sugar
½ teaspoon dry mustard
¼ teaspoon ground cinnamon

- Preheat oven to 160° C (325° F).
- Place beans in large, heavy pot, add 5 cups (1.2 L) water and boil for 2 minutes.
- Add remaining ingredients with a little salt and pepper. Cover and bake for 2 hours.
- Remove from oven and stir mixture well. Return to oven, cover and bake for additional 3 hours or until beans and beef are tender. Serves 6.

Stroganoff Stew

30 g (1 ounce) onion soup mix
2 280-g (10-ounce) cans mushroom soup
910 g (2 pounds) stew meat
230 g (8 ounces) sour cream
Noodles, cooked

- Preheat oven to 140° C (275° F).
- Combine soup mix, mushroom soup and 2 soup cans water and pour over stew meat in roasting pan.
- Cover tightly and bake for 6 to 8 hours.
- When ready to serve, stir in sour cream, return mixture to oven until it heats thoroughly and serve over noodles. Serves 6.

Meat and Potato Stew

910 g (2 pounds) beef stew meat
2 425-g (15-ounce) cans new potatoes, drained
1 425-g (15-ounce) can sliced carrots, drained
2 280-g (10-ounce) cans French onion soup

- Season meat with a little salt and pepper and cook with 2 cups (500 ml) water in large pot for 1 hour.
- Add potatoes, carrots and onion soup and mix well.
- Bring to boil, reduce heat and simmer for 30 minutes. Serves 6.

Oven-Baked Beef Stew

1 tablespoon (10 g) flour
340 g (¾ pound) beef chuck, cubed
¾ cup (120 g) chopped onion
¼ teaspoon basil
2 potatoes, peeled, cubed
2 carrots, peeled, sliced
¼ cup (60 ml) dry red wine
1 280-g (10-ounce) can tomato soup

- Preheat oven to 160° C (325° F).
- Combine flour with a little salt and pepper and pat onto both sides of meat. Brown meat in large iron frypan. Transfer to large deep frypan.
- Add all remaining ingredients with 1¼ cups (310 ml) water; cover and bake for about 1 hour. Serves 4 to 6.

Pirate Stew for the Crew

If you can open cans, you can make this stew. Don't let the number of ingredients get to you. Leave something out if you get tired of opening cans, but by all means, you can handle this recipe.

1.4 kg (3 pounds) beef chuck roast, cubed
Olive oil
2 425-g (15-ounce) cans diced tomatoes
2 950-ml (32-ounce) cans V8® juice
3 425-g (15-ounce) cans green beans, drained
3 425-g (15-ounce) cans green peas, drained
2 cups okra
2 455-g (16-ounce) cans lima beans, drained
3 455-g (16-ounce) packages frozen corn
910 g (2 pounds) onion, peeled, diced
2 kg (4 pounds) potatoes, peeled, cubed
1 teaspoon dried rosemary

- Brown beef in oil in large stew pot. Add remaining ingredients with 1 L (1 quart) water and a little salt and pepper.
- Simmer all day. Remove excess fat before serving. Serves 12 to 16.

TIP: This recipe makes enough for several meals so freeze some for later.

Blue Ribbon Beef Stew

1.2 kg (2½ pounds) boneless beef chuck roast, cubed
⅓ cup (40 g) flour
1 litre carton beef stock
1 teaspoon dried thyme
2 teaspoons minced garlic
455 g (1 pound) new (red) potatoes with peel, sliced
2 large carrots, sliced
3 sticks celery, sliced
2 onions, finely chopped
280 g (10 ounces) frozen green peas

- Dredge beef in flour and 1 teaspoon salt; reserve leftover flour. Brown half beef in stew pot over medium heat for about 10 minutes and transfer to plate.
- Repeat with remaining beef. Add reserved flour to stew pot and cook, stirring constantly, for 1 minute.
- Stir in beef stock, thyme and garlic and bring to boil. Reduce heat, simmer for 50 minutes and stir occasionally.
- Add potatoes, carrots, celery and onion and cook for 30 minutes.
- Stir in green peas, a little salt and pepper; heat to boiling. Serve hot. Serves 6.

Border-Crossing Stew

680 g (1½ pounds) round steak, cubed
2 onions, chopped
½ litre carton beef stock
1 425-g (15-ounce) can stewed tomatoes
1 teaspoon paprika
3 chopped green chillies
3 baking potatoes, peeled, cubed
2 teaspoons minced garlic
2 teaspoons ground cumin

- Brown cubed steak and onion in stew pot, cook for 10 minutes and stir often.
- Mix in beef stock, tomatoes, green chillies, potatoes, garlic, cumin, 1 cup (250 ml) water and a little salt and pepper.
- Cover and cook on medium-low heat for 35 minutes or until potatoes are tender. Serves 6.

Steakhouse Stew

455 g (1 pound) boneless beef sirloin steak, cubed
Olive oil
1 425-g (15-ounce) can stewed tomatoes
1 280-g (10-ounce) can French onion soup
1 280-g (10-ounce) can tomato soup
455 g (16 ounces) frozen stew vegetables, thawed

- Cook steak in frypan with a little oil until juices evaporate. Transfer to stew pot or roasting pan.
- Add 1 cup (250 ml) water, tomatoes, soups and vegetables and heat to boiling. Reduce heat to low and simmer for 35 minutes. Serves 6.

Green Chilli Stew Pot (Caldillo)

Caldillo is a traditional Mexican dish served on special occasions.

910 g (2 pounds) round steak, cubed
Canola oil
2 onions, chopped
2 potatoes, peeled, diced
2 cloves garlic, minced
6–8 fresh green chillies, roasted, peeled, seeded, diced

- Sprinkle round steak with 1 tablespoon (15 ml) salt; heat oil in large frypan and brown meat. Put onions, potatoes and garlic in same frypan and cook until onions are translucent.
- Pour all ingredients from frypan into large stew pot. Add chillies, 1 teaspoon salt and ½ teaspoon pepper and enough water to cover.
- Bring to boil, lower heat and simmer for 1 to 2 hours or until meat and potatoes are tender. Serves 6.

According to an old Spanish proverb, 'Of soup and love, soup is better'.

Cattle Drive Chilli Stew

1.4 kg (3 pounds) stew meat
3 tablespoons (45 ml) olive oil
1 medium onion, chopped
3 sticks celery, chopped
2 425-g (15-ounce) cans stewed tomatoes with liquid
1 teaspoon paprika
1 litre carton beef stock
280 g (10 ounces) frozen corn kernels
1 cup (240 g) diced, fresh green chillies

- Brown stew meat on all sides in large frypan with oil and transfer to large stew pot.
- Sauté onion and celery in frypan drippings until translucent and pour drippings and vegetables into stew pot.
- Stir in tomatoes, paprika, beef stock, corn, chillies, 2 teaspoons salt and ¼ teaspoon pepper and bring to boil.
- Reduce heat and simmer for 2 hours or until stew meat is tender. Serves 8.

TIP: If soup is too thin, add ¼ cup (15 g) instant mashed potato flakes.

Did you know that lettuce loves fat? Fat can be removed from hot soup by floating a large lettuce leaf on the surface.

Chilli-Soup Warmer

1 280-g (10-ounce) can tomato condensed soup
1 280-g (10-ounce) can chunky beef soup
1 280-g (10-ounce) can chilli
½ litre carton beef stock
Crackers

- Combine soups, chilli and stock in saucepan. Add amount of water to produce desired thickness of soup.
- Heat and serve hot with crackers. Serves 4 to 6.

Easy Chunky Chilli

910 g (2 pounds) premium-cut stew meat
1½ cups (375 ml) beef stock
1 onion, chopped
3 425-g (15-ounce) cans diced tomatoes
2 chopped green chillies
2 425-g (15-ounce) cans borlotti beans with liquid
1½ tablespoons (10 g) chilli powder
2 teaspoons ground cumin
1 teaspoon oregano

- If stew meat is in fairly large chunks, cut each chunk in half. Brown stew meat in large frypan and add all remaining ingredients.
- Bring to boil, reduce heat and cook on low for 1 hour. Serves 6.

Cadillac Chilli

680 g (1½ pounds) lean minced beef
910 g (2 pounds) diced beef
1 onion, chopped
Olive oil
1 425-g (15-ounce) can tomato soup
1 280-g (10-ounce) can diced tomatoes
2 chopped green chillies
4 tablespoons (25 g) ground cumin
1 teaspoon oregano
2 tablespoons (15 g) chilli powder
1 425-g (15-ounce) can borlotti beans with liquid

- Combine meats and onion in a little oil in large roasting pan and brown.
- Add tomato soup, tomatoes, green chillies, cumin, oregano, chilli powder, 2 cups (500 ml) water and a little salt.
- Bring to a boil, reduce heat and simmer for 2 hours.
- Add beans and heat until thoroughly hot. Serves 6.

Before the invention of spoons, meat and vegetables in soups were eaten from a shared bowl and people used their hands to pick the pieces out of the liquid. The better-equipped diners used knives to spear the foods.

Beefy Bean Chilli

910 g (2 pounds) lean minced beef
3 sticks celery, sliced
1 onion, chopped
1 capsicum, seeded, chopped
2 teaspoons minced garlic
1 425-g (15-ounce) can tomato soup
3 tablespoons (30 g) chilli powder
2 425-g (15-ounce) cans borlotti beans with liquid
1–2 cups (55–110 g) crushed corn chips

- Brown and cook beef in large soup pot over medium heat until meat crumbles.
- Add celery, onion, capsicum and minced garlic. Cook for 5 minutes or until vegetables are tender, but not brown.
- Stir in tomato soup, chilli powder, 2 cups (500 ml) water and a little salt and pepper and mix well.
- Bring mixture to a boil, reduce heat and simmer for 35 minutes.
- Add beans during last 15 minutes of cooking time.
- Ladle into individual serving bowls and top each serving with several tablespoons crushed corn chips. Serves 6.

Baked Chilli

1½ cups (185 g) dried borlotti beans
680 g (1½ pounds) beef round steak, cubed
3 onions, finely chopped
3 teaspoons minced garlic
3 230-g (8-ounce) cans tomato soup
3 tablespoons (30 g) chilli powder
1 tablespoon (15 ml) ground cumin
½ teaspoon cayenne pepper
230 g (8 ounces) shredded cheddar cheese

- Preheat oven to 160° C (325° F).
- Heat beans and 6 cups (1.4 L) water to boiling in large, heavy pot and boil for 2 minutes.
- Stir in all remaining ingredients except cheese, cover and bake for about 3 hours.
- Remove from oven and stir well. Return to oven and bake for additional 1 hour.
- Garnish each individual bowl with cheese. Serves 6 to 8.

Hearty Beef Chilli

3 tablespoons (45 ml) olive oil
910 g (2 pounds) round steak, cubed
2 onions, chopped
4 cloves garlic, minced
¼ cup (65 g) tomato paste
2–4 canned jalapeno chillies, stemmed, seeded, minced
3 tablespoons (30 g) chilli powder
1 teaspoon oregano
1 teaspoon ground cumin
2 425-g (15-ounce) cans diced tomatoes with liquid
1 cup (250 ml) beef stock
2 chopped green chillies
1 425-g (15-ounce) can borlotti beans, drained

- Heat 1 tablespoon (15 ml) oil in soup pot and brown beef. Transfer meat to bowl and set aside.
- Heat remaining 2 tablespoons (30 ml) oil in soup pot and add onion and garlic. Cook for about 3 minutes, stir in tomato paste, jalapeno chillies, chilli powder, 1 teaspoon each of salt and pepper, oregano and cumin.
- Add tomatoes, meat, beef stock, 1 cup (250 ml) water and green chillies.
- Bring to boil, reduce heat and simmer for 2 hours or until meat is tender and chilli thickens.
- Stir in beans and continue simmering for about 20 minutes. Serves 6.

TIP: If you like it extra hot, leave the seeds and veins in the jalapeno chillies. If you take the seeds out, rubber gloves will protect your hands from the juices.

Chilli, New Mexico-Style

This New Mexico chilli is also called 'Chilli con Carne'.

Canola oil
910 g (2 pounds) chuck or pork roast, cubed
1 litre carton beef stock
4–5 dried chipotle chillies, ground
4–6 cloves garlic, minced
3 tablespoons (30 g) paprika
1 teaspoon ground cumin
1 tablespoon (15 ml) oregano

- Heat oil in large frypan or large, heavy pot and brown meat on all sides.
- Add beef stock and ground chillies and bring to a boil. Reduce heat, simmer for about 2 hours and stir occasionally.
- Add garlic, paprika, cumin, oregano and 1 teaspoon salt.
- Cover and simmer for 15 minutes. Stir occasionally and skim grease. Serves 6.

Taco Chilli

910 g (2 pounds) very lean stew meat
½ litre carton beef stock
2 425-g (15-ounce) cans stewed tomatoes
2 teaspoons paprika
30 g (1 ounce) taco seasoning mix
2 425-g (15-ounce) cans borlotti beans with liquid
1 425-g (15-ounce) can corn kernels with liquid
230 g (8 ounces) shredded cheddar cheese

- Cut large pieces of stew meat in half and brown in large frypan.
- Combine stew meat, stock, tomatoes, paprika, taco seasoning mix, beans, corn and ¾ cup (175 ml) water in stew pot.
- Bring to boil, reduce heat and simmer for 1 hour or until meat is tender. Sprinkle cheese on top of each serving. Serves 8.

TIP: For garnish top each serving with chopped spring onions.

Spiked Chilli

2 tablespoons (30 ml) olive oil
2 onions, chopped
2 cloves garlic, minced
455 g (1 pound) lean boneless beef, cubed
455 g (1 pound) lean boneless pork, cubed
6 fresh or canned jalapeno chillies, seeded, minced
1 teaspoon dried, crushed oregano
1 teaspoon ground cumin
½ cup (125 ml) dry red wine

- Rinse jalapeno chillies, remove stems, seeds and veins and place in saucepan with 2 cups (500 ml) water. Bring to boil, turn off heat and let stand, covered for 30 minutes.
- Pour jalapeno chillies with liquid into blender and process until smooth.
- Heat oil in soup pot and sauté onion, garlic and meats until meat is light brown. Add 1 teaspoon salt, oregano, cumin, wine and chilli puree.
- Bring to boil, reduce heat, cover and simmer for 2 hours.
- Uncover and simmer for about 30 minutes or until chilli thickens slightly. Serves 6.

Chilli Verde con Carne

'Chilli con carne' means chilli with meat. Verde refers to the fresh green chillies.

910 g–1.4 kg (2–3 pounds) sirloin or tenderloin, cubed
½ cup (115 g) butter
2 onions, chopped
4–6 cloves garlic, minced
8–10 fresh whole green chillies, peeled, seeded, chopped
1 tablespoon (15 ml) ground cumin
2 teaspoons oregano

- Brown sirloin in butter in large frypan. Reduce heat to low and add all remaining ingredients plus 1 cup (250 ml) water and 1 teaspoon each of salt and pepper. Cover and simmer for about 2 to 3 hours.
- Stir occasionally and add ½ to 1 cup (125 to 250 ml) water if necessary. Remove cover, taste for flavour and adjust seasonings, if needed. Serves 6.

TIP: To save time, chilli powder may be used instead of roasting fresh green chillies, but the flavour of fresh chillies is the secret to the best chilli.

A Bowl of Red

Proper name for Real Texas Chilli, make no beans about it. At the first Original Terlingua International Cook-Off in Terlingua, Texas in 1966, Frank X. Tolbert and Wick Fowler gave real Texas chilli the name, 'Bowl of Red'.

½ cup (125 ml) beef suet or canola oil
1.4 kg (3 pounds) sirloin steak, cubed
4–5 dried chipotle chillies, ground
1–2 whole jalapeno chillies
4–6 cloves garlic, minced
½ cup (50 g) paprika
2 tablespoons (15 g) ground cumin
2 tablespoons (15 g) cornflour, optional

- Heat suet in frypan until fat separates from connective tissue or heat vegetable oil for healthier cooking. Remove suet and brown sirloin on all sides.
- Pour sirloin and oil from frypan in large pot or roasting pan. Add ground chillies, 1 whole jalapeno chilli and enough water to be about 5 cm (2 inches) above meat.
- Bring water to boil, reduce heat and simmer for about 2 to 3 hours. Stir occasionally and skim grease.
- Add garlic, paprika, cumin and 1 tablespoon (15 ml) salt, cover and simmer for additional 1 hour. Stir occasionally and skim grease.
- Check seasonings and if not hot enough, add whole jalapeno chilli. Add cornflour if chilli is too thin and simmer for additional 30 minutes to 1 hour. Serves 6.

Championship Chilli

Real chilli is worth the effort!

Olive oil
1.4–1.6 kg (3–3½ pounds) stew meat
1 onion, chopped
1 425-g (15-ounce) can tomato soup
10–12 tablespoons (65–80 g) dried chillies, ground
1–2 tablespoons (5–15 g) ground cumin
1 tablespoon (15 ml) oregano
1–2 jalapeno chillies
Crackers

- Brown stew meat and onion in a little oil in large pot or roasting pan.
- Add tomato soup, ground chillies, cumin, oregano, 1 tablespoon (15 ml) salt and enough water to be 5 cm (2 inches) above meat and bring to a boil. Reduce heat and simmer for about 2 hours. Stir occasionally.
- Taste for seasonings and add whole jalapeno chilli if more 'hot' is needed. Simmer for an additional 1 hour.
- Serve immediately with crackers or wait until the next day to serve. Some people believe real chilli needs time for flavours to blend. Serves 6 to 8.

Big-Time Chilli

You know the chilli's good when it makes your nose run.

2 onions, chopped
¼ cup (60 ml) olive oil
1.4 kg (3 pounds) lean minced beef
1 425-g (15-ounce) can diced tomatoes
1 170-g (6-ounce) can tomato paste
¾ teaspoon cayenne pepper
4–6 tablespoons (25–40 g) chilli powder
2 teaspoons ground cumin
1 tablespoon (15 ml) paprika

- Sauté onions in oil and brown beef in roasting pan.
- Mix in all remaining ingredients with 2 teaspoons salt and bring to a boil. Reduce heat and simmer for 3 hours.
- Stir several times and add water, if needed. Serves 6.

Venison Chilli

115 g (¼ pound) salt pork, quartered
1.1 kg (2½ pounds) ground venison
2 onions, chopped
1 425-g (15-ounce) can stewed tomatoes
¾ cup (175 ml) red wine
2 teaspoons minced garlic
3 tablespoons (30 g) chilli powder
¾ teaspoon dried oregano
1 teaspoon ground cumin

- Brown salt pork in soup pot over medium heat.
- Add venison and onion, cook over medium-high heat until venison browns and crumbles and stir often.
- Stir in tomatoes, wine, garlic, chilli powder, oregano, cumin, 1 cup (250 ml) water and a little salt.
- Bring to boil, reduce heat and simmer for 1 hour, stirring occasionally. Remove salt pork before serving. Serves 6.

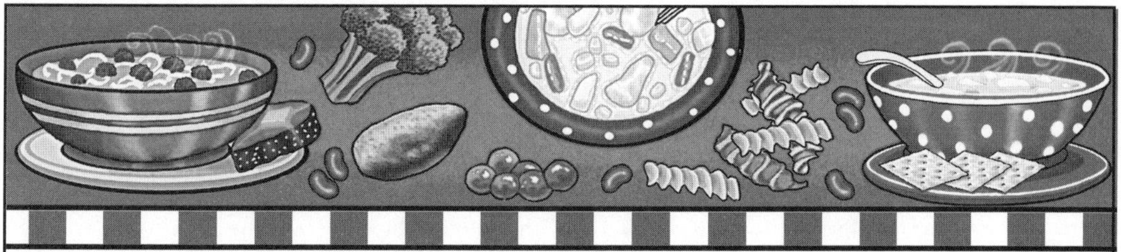

Perfect Pork Pleasers

Try these recipes loaded with ham, sausage and bacon and blended with hearty vegetables, beans, peas, rice and pasta.

Perfect Pork Pleasers Contents

Ham and Black Bean Soup

Half of the ingredients listed for this recipe are seasonings, so don't be scared about time and effort for this soup. It doesn't take much time to measure seasonings.

2 cups (250 g) dried black beans
1 cup (280 g) cooked, diced ham
1 onion, chopped
1 carrot, chopped
2 sticks celery, chopped
3 jalapeno chillies, seeded, chopped
1 litre carton chicken stock
2 teaspoons ground cumin
2 tablespoons (2 g) snipped fresh coriander
1 teaspoon oregano
1 teaspoon chilli powder
½–1 teaspoon cayenne pepper
230 g (8 ounces) sour cream

- Wash beans, soak overnight and drain.
- Except for sour cream, place all ingredients and 1 teaspoon salt with 10 cups (2 L) water in large, heavy soup pot.
- Bring to boil, reduce heat and simmer for 3 hours or until beans are tender. Add more water as needed and stir occasionally. Make sure there is enough water in pot to make soup consistency, so not too thick.
- Place few cups at a time in food processor (using steel blade) or blender and puree until smooth.
- Add sour cream and reheat soup. Serve in individual bowls. Serves 8.

Hearty Bean and Ham Soup

What a great dinner for a cold winter night!

1 415-g (15-ounce) can sliced carrots, drained
1 cup (200 g) chopped celery
1 cup (140 g) seeded, chopped green capsicum
¼ cup (60 g) butter
2–3 cups (280–420 g) cooked, diced ham
2 425-g (15-ounce) cans cannellini beans with liquid
2 425-g (15-ounce) cans borlotti beans with liquid
1 litre carton chicken stock
2 teaspoons chilli powder

- Cook carrots, celery and capsicum in soup pot with butter for about 8 minutes until tender but crisp.
- Add diced ham, cannellini beans, borlotti beans, chicken stock, chilli powder and a little salt and pepper. Boil and stir constantly for 3 minutes. Reduce heat and simmer for 15 minutes. Serves 8.

Borlotti Bean Soup

2 455-g (1-pound) packages dry borlotti beans
1 smoked ham hock or 2 cups (280 g) cooked, chopped ham

- Wash beans, cover with cold water in soup pot and soak overnight.
- Drain beans, cover with water and bring to boil.
- Add ham, reduce heat and simmer slowly for 3 to 4 hours. (You may need to add more water.)
- When beans are tender, remove 2 to 3 cups (250 to 370 g) beans and smash with potato masher.
- Return to pot and season with salt. Serves 6.

Cannellini Bean Soup

This soup tastes great with cornbread.

3 425-g (15-ounce) cans cannellini beans with liquid
½ litre carton chicken stock
1 cup (140 g) cooked, chopped ham
1 large onion, chopped
½ teaspoon garlic powder

- Combine all ingredients with 1 cup (250 ml) water in large saucepan and bring to boil.
- Simmer until onion is tender but crisp and serve hot. Serves 6.

Frijole Soup

1½ pounds (680 g) dried borlotti beans
5 slices thick sliced bacon, cut in pieces
2 onions, chopped
1 teaspoon garlic powder
½ teaspoon thyme
½ teaspoon oregano
½ teaspoon cayenne pepper
Flour tortillas
Butter

- Wash beans, place in large soup pot and cover with water. Soak overnight and drain.
- Cook bacon and onions in frypan for about 5 minutes.
- Transfer with pan drippings to soup pot. Bring to boil and add all seasonings.
- Lower heat and cook for 4 hours. Add hot water when liquid goes below original level.
- When beans are done, remove about half of beans and mash beans with potato masher or process in blender.
- Return to pot and add 1 tablespoon (15 ml) salt.
- Serve with hot flour tortillas and butter. Serves 4.

The earliest evidence of humans eating soup is 6,000 B.C.

Good Ol' Bean Soup

3 tablespoons (45 ml) olive oil
1 cup (110 g) shredded carrots
1 onion, chopped
1 red capsicum, chopped
1 green capsicum, chopped
1 litre carton chicken stock
2 425-g (15-ounce) cans borlotti beans with liquid
2 cups (280 g) cooked, diced ham

- Combine oil, carrots, onions and capsicums in soup pot and cook for 10 minutes.
- Add stock, borlotti beans, ham and ½ cup (125 ml) water.
- Bring to boil, reduce heat and simmer for 15 minutes. Serves 6.

Ham Bone Soup

2 cups (525 g) dried cannellini beans
230 g (½ pound) ham hock

- Cover beans with water and soak overnight.
- Drain and pour beans in large soup pot with 6 cups (1.4 L) water.
- Cook with ham hocks for 2 to 3 hours or until tender.
- Season with a little salt and pepper. Serves 4.

Tomato and White Bean Soup

2 tablespoons (30 ml) olive oil
1 onion, chopped
1 green capsicum, seeded, chopped
1 425-g (15-ounce) can diced tomatoes
1 litre carton chicken stock
2 425-g (15-ounce) cans cannellini beans, rinsed, drained
1½ cups (210 g) cooked, cubed ham
½ cup (30 g) chopped fresh parsley

- Combine olive oil, onion and capsicum in large saucepan and sauté for 5 minutes and stir constantly.
- Stir in tomatoes, stock, cannellini beans and ham and bring to boil. Reduce heat and simmer for 10 minutes.
- Pour into individual soup bowls and sprinkle parsley on top. Serves 4.

Easy Cannellini Soup

4 slices bacon
1 onion, chopped
1 red capsicum, seeded, chopped
2 teaspoons minced garlic
1½ litres chicken stock
1 425-g (15-ounce) can cannellini beans, drained
1 teaspoon dried parsley

- Fry bacon in soup pot, drain and save drippings in soup pot. Crumble bacon and set aside. Add onion, capsicum and garlic to drippings and sauté for 5 minutes, stirring occasionally.
- Stir in chicken stock, beans, ½ teaspoon pepper, parsley and a little salt. Bring to boil, reduce heat and simmer for 20 minutes.
- Sprinkle crumbled bacon over each serving of soup. Serves 4.

Soup with an Attitude

1 litre carton chicken stock
3 baked potatoes, peeled, grated
2 onions, finely chopped
3 sticks celery, sliced
1 230-g (8-ounce) can peas, drained
2 chopped green chillies
3 cups (420 g) cooked, chopped ham
455 g (16 ounces) cubed cheddar cheese
500 ml (1 pint) unthickened cream

- Combine stock, potatoes, onions, celery, peas, green chillies and ham in soup pot.
- While stirring, bring to a boil, reduce heat to medium-low and simmer for 30 minutes.
- Add cheese and cook on medium heat, stir constantly until cheese melts.
- Stir in cream and continue cooking until soup is thoroughly hot; do not boil. Serves 8.

To make a good base for your soup, you can use any of the following: canned soups (such as cream of mushroom soup), canned tomatoes, tomato juice, commercial chicken stock, homemade stocks, commercial soup bases, clam or seafood stock and the addition of some bacon.

Cabbage-Ham Soup

1 cup shredded white cabbage
1 cup shredded red cabbage
1 cup shredded carrot
1 onion, chopped
1 red capsicum, seeded, chopped
1 teaspoon minced garlic
1 litre carton chicken stock
1 425-g (15-ounce) can stewed tomatoes
2 cups (280 g) cooked, cubed ham
¼ cup (55 g) brown sugar
2 tablespoons (30 ml) lemon juice

- Combine cabbage, carrot, onion, capsicum, garlic and chicken stock in large, heavy soup pot.
- Bring to boil, reduce heat and simmer for 20 minutes.
- Stir in tomatoes, ham, 1 teaspoon salt, brown sugar, lemon juice and a little pepper. Heat just until soup is thoroughly hot. Serves 6.

The Italian word 'zuppa' once described a soup served over a thick piece of bread. Throughout history, people have used bread to thicken soup and add substance to broth. Today the term 'zuppa' simply means a thick soup.

Spicy Bean Soup

1 425-g (15-ounce) can refried beans
½ litre carton chicken stock
4 chopped green chillies
2 cloves garlic, minced
2–3 jalapeno chillies, seeded, chopped
1 teaspoon chilli powder
6 slices bacon
1 bunch spring onions with tops, chopped
5 sticks celery, chopped
1 capsicum, seeded, chopped
230 g (8 ounces) shredded cheddar cheese

- Heat and whisk refried beans and chicken stock in large saucepan.
- Add green chillies, garlic, jalapeno chillies, ¼ teaspoon pepper and chilli powder and stir well. Reduce heat to low and stir occasionally.
- Fry bacon in frypan until crisp and sauté about three-fourths onions, celery and capsicum in pan drippings until onions are translucent.
- Crumble bacon and add to bean soup.
- Add onions, celery, capsicum and pan drippings and stir well.
- Bring to boil, reduce heat to low and serve immediately.
- Garnish with remaining onions and cheese. Serves 6.

Bonza Chickpea Soup

1 onion, chopped
1 red capsicum, chopped
1 green capsicum, chopped
Olive oil
455 g (1 pound) Italian sausage, cut up
½ litre carton beef stock
1 425-g (15-ounce) can Italian stewed tomatoes
2 425-g (15-ounce) cans chickpeas, rinsed, drained

- Sauté onions and capsicums in soup pot with a little oil.
- Add Italian sausage and cook until brown.
- Stir in beef stock, stewed tomatoes and chickpeas.
- Bring mixture to boil, reduce heat and simmer for about 30 minutes. Serves 6.

Lucky Pea Soup

Lucky Pea Soup is great on New Year's Day and brings good luck in the New Year.

1 onion, chopped
Olive oil
1 cup (140 g) cooked, cubed ham
2 cups black-eyed peas, soaked, rinsed
½ litre carton chicken stock
1 teaspoon minced garlic
1 teaspoon dried sage

- Sauté onion in a little oil in large saucepan. Add ham, black-eyed peas, stock, garlic and sage and cook on high heat.
- Bring to boil, reduce heat and simmer and stir occasionally for 20 minutes. Serves 4.

Split Pea Soup

This is great for leftover ham.

455 g (16 ounces) dried green split peas
1 onion, chopped
1 large potato, peeled, diced
2 sticks celery, chopped
1 cup (140 g) cooked shredded or chopped ham
1 cup (110 g) shredded carrots
1 teaspoon minced garlic
Seasoned croutons

- Sort and rinse peas and place in large, heavy soup pot. Cover with water 5 cm (2 inches) above peas and soak overnight.
- Drain, add 2 quarts (2 L) water, onion, potato, celery, ham, carrots, garlic and a little salt and pepper.
- Bring to boil, reduce heat, cover and simmer for 2 hours 30 minutes to 3 hours and stir occasionally. (If you happen to have a meaty ham bone, you can use that instead of chopped ham.)
- Cool slightly and process mixture in batches in blender until smooth.
- Return mixture to soup pot, cover and simmer for 5 minutes or until thoroughly hot.
- Garnish with seasoned croutons. Serves 6.

Split Pea and Tortellini Soup

⅓ cup (65 g) dry split peas
2 tablespoons (8 g) dried minced onion
1½ teaspoons dried basil
1 tablespoon (15 ml) minced garlic
½ cup (55 g) shredded carrots
1 280-g (10-ounce) can tomatoes
2 chopped green chillies
¾ cup (180 ml) cheese-filled tortellini
1 cup (140 g) cooked, diced ham
1 litre carton chicken stock

- Combine all ingredients in soup pot.
- Bring to boil, reduce heat and simmer for 45 minutes or until peas are tender. Serves 6.

Tomato-Bacon Soup

1 280-g (10-ounce) can tomato soup
1 400-g (14-ounce) can stewed tomatoes
3 slices bacon, fried, drained, crumbled

- Combine soup and stewed tomatoes in soup pot. Heat thoroughly.
- Pour into soup bowls, sprinkle bacon on top and serve hot. Serves 4.

Old-Fashioned Hoppin' John

4 cups black-eyed peas, soaked overnight
½ litre carton chicken stock
1 teaspoon minced garlic
½ cup (50 g) rice
2 onions, finely chopped
1 red capsicum, seeded, chopped
1½ cups (210 g) cooked, cubed ham
2 cups mustard greens (gai choy), coarsely chopped

- Combine peas, stock, 2 cups (500 ml) water, garlic, rice, onions and capsicum in soup pot and bring to boil.
- Reduce heat and simmer, stirring occasionally, until rice is tender, for about 25 to 30 minutes.
- Stir in ham and greens and cook on medium heat for 5 to 10 minutes or until soup is thoroughly hot. Serves 4.

Soup That's Soul Food

3 425-g (15-ounce) cans cannellini beans with liquid
2 onions, chopped
2 teaspoons minced garlic
3 potatoes, peeled, cubed
2 cups (280 g) cooked, diced ham
1 litre carton chicken stock
2 cups chopped turnip greens

- Place 1 can beans in shallow bowl and mash with fork. Spray large soup pot and stir in mashed beans, remaining cans of beans, onions, garlic, potatoes, ham, stock, turnip greens and a little salt and pepper. Bring to a boil and boil for 5 minutes; reduce heat to low and simmer for 45 minutes or until potatoes and greens are tender. Serve hot. Serves 6.

Potato-Sausage Soup

455 g (1 pound) pork sausages
1 cup (100 g) chopped celery
1 cup (160 g) chopped onion
2 280-g (10-ounce) cans potato soup
½ litre carton chicken stock

- Cut sausage into 2.5-cm (1-inch) diagonal slices.
- Brown sausage in large heavy soup pot, drain and place in separate bowl.
- Leave about 2 tablespoons (30 ml) sausage drippings in frypan and sauté celery and onion.
- Add potato soup, ¾ cup (175 ml) water, chicken stock and sausage.
- Bring to boil, reduce heat and simmer for 20 minutes. Serves 4.

Rich Cheese Soup

5 slices bacon
1 small onion, finely chopped
2 sticks celery, finely sliced
1 medium leek, halved lengthwise, sliced
1 litre carton chicken stock
⅔ cup (55 g) quick-cooking oats
1 cup (110 g) shredded Swiss cheese
250 ml (8 ounces) pouring cream

- Cook bacon in large saucepan until crisp, drain and crumble. Save drippings in saucepan.
- Cook onion, celery and leek in pan drippings over medium heat for 10 minutes and stir often.
- Add stock and oats. Bring to boil, reduce heat and simmer for 15 minutes. Cool slightly.
- Place half soup in blender and process until smooth. Repeat with remaining soup.
- Return all soup mixture to saucepan and stir in cheese and cream; heat until cheese melts. Do not boil.
- Ladle soup into bowls and sprinkle with crumbled bacon. Serves 4.

You can give commercial stock a little extra flavour by simmering reserved chicken or meat bones in the broth for 15 minutes. Strain the liquid and use it for your soup.

Creamed Broccoli Soup

4 slices bacon
1 small onion, minced
3 potatoes, shredded
280 g (10 ounces) frozen chopped broccoli florets
¼ cup (60 g) butter
3 tablespoons (20 g) flour
500 ml (1 pint) unthickened cream

- Fry bacon in deep frypan, drain and set aside.
- With bacon drippings still in frypan, add onion, potatoes, 2 cups (500 ml) water and 1 teaspoon salt. Cover and cook for about 10 minutes.
- Add broccoli and cook for additional 5 minutes.
- In separate large saucepan, melt butter and add flour. Stir and cook until mixture bubbles. Gradually add cream, cook and stir constantly until it thickens.
- Stir in potato-broccoli mixture and heat just until thoroughly hot. Crumble bacon and sprinkle on top of each serving. Serves 4.

Ham and Potato Soup

510 g (18 ounces) frozen hash browns thawed
1 litre carton chicken stock
3 sticks celery, finely chopped
2 280-g (10-ounce) cans cream of chicken soup
2 cups (500 ml) milk
2 cups (280 g) cooked, chopped ham
2 teaspoons minced garlic
1 teaspoon dried parsley flakes

- Combine hash browns, stock and celery in large soup pot and bring to boil. Reduce heat and simmer for 25 minutes.
- Pour in soup and milk and stir until mixture is smooth.
- Add ham, garlic, parsley and ½ teaspoon pepper.
- Bring to boil, stir constantly, immediately reduce heat and simmer for 10 minutes. Serves 6.

Bacon-Potato Soup

1 litre carton chicken stock
1 teaspoon minced garlic
2 potatoes, peeled, cubed
1 onion, finely chopped
6 slices bacon, cooked, crumbled

- Combine stock, potatoes and onion in large saucepan. Bring to a boil, reduce heat to medium-high and boil for about 10 minutes or until potatoes are tender.
- Season with a little pepper. Ladle into bowls and sprinkle with crumbled bacon. Serves 4.

Snap-Your-Fingers Potato Soup

2 280-g (10-ounce) cans creamy potato soup
1 cup (115 g) shredded cheddar cheese
3 tablespoons (10 g) bacon bits

- Heat potato soup with 1 cup (250 ml) water or milk in soup pot. Stir in cheese.
- Pour soup into soup bowls and sprinkle with bacon bits. Serves 4.

Green Chilli Soup

5 slices bacon, cut into 2.5-cm (1-inch) pieces, divided
1 onion, finely chopped
2 sticks celery, finely chopped
3 potatoes, peeled, cubed
2 chopped green chillies
1 litre carton chicken stock
500 ml (1 pint) unthickened cream

- Fry bacon pieces until half done in soup pot. Place half bacon in separate bowl and set aside.
- Add onion and celery to soup pot and cook on medium heat until onion is translucent.
- Add potatoes, green chillies, chicken stock, ½ cup (125 ml) water and ½ teaspoon each of salt and pepper.
- Cook on medium-low heat until potatoes are tender, about 15 minutes. To make soup a little thicker, mash some potatoes with fork against sides of pan.
- When ready to serve, pour in cream and heat, but do not boil.
- Microwave remaining bacon until crisp. Sprinkle bacon on top of each serving to garnish. Serves 6.

Cowboy Sausage-Bean Soup

455 g (1 pound) pork sausage meat
2 425-g (15-ounce) cans borlotti beans
2 425-g (15-ounce) cans stewed tomatoes
1 onion, chopped
¼ teaspoon garlic powder
½ teaspoon thyme
1 tablespoon (15 ml) chilli powder
¼ teaspoon dried coriander
1 large potato, peeled, diced
1 capsicum, seeded, chopped
230 g (8 ounces) cubed cheddar cheese
½ cup (60 g) shredded Colby cheese

- Brown sausage meat in large, heavy soup pot and drain fat.
- Add beans, tomatoes, 1 L (1 quart) water, onions, 1 teaspoon (5 ml) salt, garlic powder, thyme, chilli powder, coriander and ¼ teaspoon pepper.
- Bring to boil, reduce heat. Cover and simmer for 1 hour.
- Add potatoes and capsicum, cover and simmer for additional 30 minutes or until potatoes are soft, but not mushy.
- Stir in cheddar cheese and heat just until it melts.
- To serve, sprinkle each serving with Colby cheese. Serves 6.

Sausage-Tortellini Soup

455 g (1 pound) Italian sausage meat
1 onion, chopped
3 sticks celery, sliced
1 litre carton beef stock
½ teaspoon dried basil
1 425-g (15-ounce) can sliced carrots, drained
1 medium zucchini, halved, sliced
1 425-g (15-ounce) can Italian stewed tomatoes
255 g (9 ounces) refrigerated meat-filled tortellini
Mozzarella cheese

- Cook and stir sausage meat, onion and celery in soup pot on medium heat until sausage is light brown.
- Drain and stir in beef stock, 1½ cups (375 ml) water, basil, carrots, zucchini, tomatoes, pasta and a little salt and pepper.
- Bring to boil, reduce heat and simmer for 20 minutes or until pasta is tender.
- Ladle into individual soup bowls and sprinkle each serving with cheese. Serves 6.

Supper Sausage Soup

455 g (1 pound) bulk Italian sausage meat
1 onion, chopped
1 red capsicum, chopped
1 green capsicum, chopped
2 425-g (15-ounce) cans stewed tomatoes
1 115-g (4-ounce) can sliced mushrooms, drained
1 litre carton beef stock
¾ cup (200 g) hot salsa
1 teaspoon dried basil
1 teaspoon sugar
Shredded mozzarella cheese

- Brown and cook sausage meat, onions and capsicums in soup pot until sausage crumbles.
- Stir in tomatoes, mushrooms, stock, salsa, basil, sugar and a little salt and pepper.
- Bring to boil, reduce heat and simmer for about 15 minutes.
- Before serving, sprinkle a little cheese over each serving. Serves 6.

If your sauce, soup or stew is too salty, add a peeled potato into the pot, and it will absorb the extra salt.

Wild Rice and Ham Soup

170 g (6 ounces) long grain-wild rice
1 onion, chopped
1 red capsicum, chopped
1 green capsicum, chopped
1 280-g (10-ounce) can cream of celery soup
1 litre carton chicken stock
2 cups (280 g) cooked, diced ham
3 cups black-eyed peas, soaked overnight
230 g (8 ounces) sour cream

- Cook rice according to package directions.
- Combine rice, onions, capsicums, celery soup, stock, ham and black-eyed peas in soup pot.
- Bring to a boil, reduce heat and simmer for 20 minutes.
- When ready to serve, stir in sour cream. Serves 6.

Southern Gumbo

This is great for leftover ham and no one will know it's a 'leftover' meal.

2 tablespoons (30 g) butter
2 tablespoons (15 g) flour
½ litre carton chicken stock
1 425-g (15-ounce) can diced tomatoes
1 cup (140 g) cooked, shredded ham
2 cups (200 g) fresh, sliced okra

- Mix butter and flour in large saucepan. Cook over medium heat and stir constantly until a paste-like roux turns light brown. Stir in stock, tomatoes, ham and okra and bring to a boil.
- Reduce heat to low and simmer for 25 minutes, stirring often, until gumbo thickens slightly. Serves 4.

Sausage-Vegetable Soup

455 g (1 pound) bulk Italian sausage meat
2 onions, chopped
2 teaspoons minced garlic
30 g (1 ounce) beef soup mix
1 425-g (15-ounce) can sliced carrots, drained
2 425-g (15-ounce) cans Italian stewed tomatoes
2 425-g (15-ounce) cans chickpeas, drained
1 cup (105 g) elbow macaroni

- Brown sausage meat, onions and garlic in large soup pot. Drain and add 4 cups (1 L) water, soup mix, carrots, tomatoes and chickpeas. Bring to boil, reduce heat and simmer for 25 minutes.
- Add pasta and continue cooking for additional 15 to 20 minutes or until pasta is tender. Serves 6.

Ham and Fresh Okra Soup

1 ham hock
1 280-g (10-ounce) can butter beans or lima beans
680 g (1½ pounds) cooked, cubed ham or chicken
1 425-g (15-ounce) can stewed tomatoes
3 cups (215 g) small, whole okra
2 large onions, diced
Rice, cooked

- Boil ham hock in 1.5 L (1½ quarts) water for about 1 hour 30 minutes in soup pot.
- Add remaining ingredients with a little salt and pepper and simmer for additional 1 hour.
- Remove ham hock and serve over rice. Serves 6.

Easy Pork Tenderloin Stew

Cornbread is really good with this stew.

2–3 cups (280–420 g) cooked, cubed pork
1 340-g (12-ounce) jar pork gravy
¼ cup (70 g) chilli sauce
455 g (16 ounces) frozen stew vegetables

- Combine cubed pork, gravy, chilli sauce, stew vegetables and ½ cup (125 ml) water in stew pot.
- Boil for 2 minutes, reduce heat and simmer for 10 minutes. Serves 4.

Pancho Villa Stew

455 g (1 pound) smoked sausage
3 cups (420 g) cooked, diced ham
1½ litres chicken stock
1 425-g (15-ounce) can diced tomatoes with liquid
6 chopped green chillies
1 large onion, chopped
1 teaspoon garlic powder
2 teaspoons ground cumin
2 teaspoons cocoa
1 teaspoon dried oregano
2 425-g (15-ounce) cans borlotti beans with liquid
1 425-g (15-ounce) can cannellini beans with liquid
1 230-g (8-ounce) can corn kernels, drained
Flour tortillas or cornbread

- Cut sausage into 1.2-cm (½-inch) slices.
- Combine sausage, ham, stock, tomatoes, green chillies, onion, garlic powder, cumin, cocoa, oregano and ½ teaspoon salt in roasting pan.
- Bring to boil, reduce heat and simmer for 45 minutes.
- Add borlotti beans, cannellini beans and corn and bring to boil. Reduce heat and simmer for additional 15 minutes.
- Serve with buttered flour tortillas or cornbread. Serves 8.

Hearty Ranch-Bean Stew

230 g (½ pound) lean beef stew meat
455 g (1 pound) pork loin, cubed
2 tablespoons (30 ml) olive oil
½ litre carton beef stock
2 425-g (15-ounce) cans baked beans
2 425-g (15-ounce) cans stewed tomatoes
2 teaspoons paprika
1 310-g (11-ounce) can corn
1 red capsicum seeded, chopped
1 green capsicum, seeded, chopped
10 g (0.4 ounce) French onion soup mix
1 teaspoon ground cumin
1 jalapeno chilli
Crushed corn chips

- Brown beef and pork meats in hot oil in heavy stew pot and season with a little salt and pepper. Add beef stock and heat to boiling. Reduce heat and simmer for 30 minutes.

- Add beans, tomatoes, paprika, corn, capsicums, soup mix, cumin, chilli and ½ cup (125 ml) water; simmer for about 20 minutes.

- Before serving, remove chilli. Serve in bowl with handful of crushed chips on top of each serving. Serves 6.

TIP: If you don't want to use a jalapeno chilli, just add chilli powder to taste.

Pecos Pork Stew

910 g (2 pounds) boneless pork shoulder, cubed
Olive oil
1 onion, chopped
1 red capsicum, seeded, chopped
1 green capsicum, seeded, chopped
2 cloves garlic, minced
¼ cup (5 g) fresh chopped coriander
3 tablespoons (30 g) chilli powder
1 litre carton chicken stock
2 cups (300 g) peeled, cubed potatoes
455 g (16 ounces) frozen corn
Cornbread

- Brown meat in a little oil in large roasting pan.
- Stir in onions, capsicums, garlic, coriander, chilli powder, 1 teaspoon salt and chicken stock.
- Cover and cook on medium heat for about 45 minutes or until pork is tender.
- Add potatoes and corn. Bring to boil, turn heat down to medium and cook for additional 30 minutes. Serve with cornbread. Serves 6.

Southwest Pork Stew

2 tablespoons (30 ml) olive oil
2 onions, chopped
1 green capsicum, seeded, chopped
3 teaspoons minced garlic
910 g (2 pounds) pork tenderloin, cubed
1 litre carton chicken stock
2 baking potatoes, peeled, cubed
2 425-g (15-ounce) cans stewed tomatoes
1 425-g (15-ounce) can chickpeas, drained
4 teaspoons chilli powder
1 teaspoon ground cumin
1 tablespoon (15 ml) lime juice

- Place oil in stew pot and sauté onion, capsicum and garlic for 5 minutes.
- Add cubed pork and chicken stock and bring to boil. Reduce heat and simmer for 25 minutes.
- Add potatoes and cook for additional 15 minutes or until potatoes are tender.
- Stir in tomatoes, chickpeas, chilli powder, cumin, lime juice and a little salt. Heat just until stew is thoroughly hot. Serves 6.

Polish Vegetable Stew

Olive oil
1 onion, sliced
2 carrots, peeled, sliced
1 capsicum, seeded, chopped
2 425-g (15-ounce) cans stewed tomatoes
2 425-g (15-ounce) cans new potatoes, drained, quartered
455 g (1 pound) Polish sausage, sliced
2 cups shredded cabbage

- Place a little oil in large stew pot. Cook onion, carrots and capsicum for 3 minutes or until tender but crisp.
- Add tomatoes and ½ cup (125 ml) water; stir well.
- Stir potatoes and sausage into soup mixture. Bring to boil, reduce heat and simmer for 10 minutes.
- Stir in cabbage and cook on medium heat for additional 8 minutes, stirring occasionally. Serves 6.

Black Bean Stew Dinner

455 g (1 pound) pork sausages, thinly sliced
2 onions, chopped
3 sticks celery, sliced
Olive oil
4 cups black beans, soaked overnight, rinsed
2 280-g (10-ounce) cans diced tomatoes
4 chopped green chillies
1 litre carton chicken stock

- Place sausage slices, onion and celery in stew pot with a little oil, cook until sausage is light brown and onion is soft and drain.
- Add beans, tomatoes, green chillies and stock.
- Bring to boil, reduce heat and simmer for 30 minutes.
- Take out about 2 cups (500 ml) stew mixture, pour into food processor and pulse until almost smooth.
- Return mixture to pot and stir to thicken stew. Return heat to high until stew is thoroughly hot. Serves 6.

Ham and Sausage Stew

3 cups (420 g) cooked, diced ham
455 g (1 pound) Polish sausage, sliced
1½ litres chicken stock
2 425-g (15-ounce) cans stewed tomatoes
1 tablespoon (15 ml) ground cumin
Olive oil
2 425-g (15-ounce) cans cannellini beans with liquid
2 425-g (15-ounce) cans corn kernels, drained
Flour tortillas

- Combine ham, sausage, chicken stock, tomatoes, cumin and a little salt in large roasting pan.
- Add a little oil and cook on high heat for about 5 minutes.
- Add cannellini beans and corn, reduce heat and simmer for 35 minutes.
- Serve with warmed, buttered flour tortillas. Serves 8.

Did you know ice cubes love fat? Eliminate fat from soup by dropping ice cubes into your soup pot. As you stir, the fat will cling to the cubes.

Turnip Greens Stew

2 cups (280 g) cooked, chopped ham
1 litre carton chicken stock
3 cups chopped turnip greens
1 onion, chopped
1 red capsicum, chopped
1 green capsicum, chopped
280 g (10 ounces) frozen corn
1 teaspoon sugar

- Combine all ingredients with 1 teaspoon pepper in large stew pot.
- Bring to boil; cover, reduce heat and simmer, stirring occasionally, for 25 minutes. Serves 6 to 8.

Southern Turnip Greens Stew

3 cups chopped turnip greens
1 onion, chopped
1 red capsicum, chopped
1 green capsicum, chopped
2 cups (280 g) cooked, chopped ham
1 litre carton chicken stock

- Combine turnip greens, onions, capsicums, ham, chicken stock and 1 teaspoon pepper in stew pot.
- Bring to boil, reduce heat, cover and simmer for 30 minutes. Serves 4 to 6.

Ham and Lentil Stew

30 g (1 ounce) onion-mushroom soup mix
½ litre carton chicken stock
1 cup (125 g) lentils, rinsed, drained
1 cup (185 g) brown rice
2 cups (320 g) chopped onion
2 cups (200 g) chopped celery
2 425-g (15-ounce) cans diced tomatoes with liquid
1 425-g (15-ounce) can sliced carrots, drained
2 cups (280 g) cooked, cubed ham
1 tablespoon (15 ml) cider vinegar

- Combine soup mix, chicken stock, lentils, rice, onions, celery and 2 cups (500 ml) water in stew pot.
- Bring to boil, reduce heat and simmer for 45 minutes.
- Stir in tomatoes, carrots, ham and vinegar and cook on medium heat until mixture is thoroughly hot. Serves 6.

Posole

Posole is a traditional dish made famous in Jalisco, Mexico. Families pass recipes through generations and all have opinions about the ingredients for their special dish. This recipe is a faster version than the typical all-day soups or stews.

455 g (1 pound) boneless pork shoulder, cubed
¼ cup (30 g) flour
¼ cup (60 ml) olive oil
1 clove garlic, minced
1 onion, chopped
1 425-g (15-ounce) can borlotti beans with liquid
3 chopped green chillies
1–2 teaspoons fresh, chopped coriander
½ teaspoon cayenne pepper
1 litre carton chicken stock
1 425-g (15-ounce) can chickpeas, drained
1½ teaspoons dried oregano leaves

- Dredge pork in flour and brown in oil in soup pot.
- Add garlic and onion, sauté until onion is translucent and drain excess oil.
- Stir in beans, green chillies, coriander, cayenne pepper and chicken stock.
- Bring to boil, cover and simmer for about 45 minutes.
- Stir in chickpeas, 1 teaspoon salt and oregano leaves and simmer for 15 to 20 minutes. Serves 6.

Quick-Step Posole

680–908 g (1½–2 pounds) boneless pork shoulder, cubed
¼ cup (30 g) flour
2 tablespoons (30 ml) olive oil
2 onions, chopped
1 clove garlic, minced
2 sticks celery, chopped
1 230-g (8-ounce) can chickpeas, drained
1 280-g (10-ounce) bottle red chilli sauce

- Season pork with 1 teaspoon (5 ml) salt and ½ teaspoon (2 ml) pepper and dredge in flour on all sides.
- Heat oil in large saucepan and brown pork. Add onions, garlic and celery; cook until onions are translucent.
- Add chickpeas and red chilli sauce to saucepan. Cover and cook on low for about 40 minutes or until pork is tender. Stir occasionally. Serves 6.

Easy Veggie-Ham Chowder

1 carrot, grated
2 sticks celery, sliced
1 onion, chopped
1 130-g (4.5-ounce) box instant mashed-potato mix
3 cups (750 ml) milk
2 cups (280 g) cooked, cubed ham
Sharp cheddar cheese

- Combine 2¾ cups (675 ml) water with carrot, celery, onion and potato mix in soup pot.
- Bring to boil, reduce heat, cover and simmer for 20 minutes.
- Stir in milk, mix well and bring to boil. Simmer for 2 minutes and stir in ham.
- Before serving, garnish with sharp cheddar cheese. Serves 8.

Ham and Corn Chowder

3 medium potatoes, cubed
1 litre carton chicken stock
2 sticks celery, chopped
1 onion, chopped
Olive oil
4 tablespoons (30 g) flour
500 ml (1 pint) light cream
½ teaspoon cayenne pepper
1 425-g (15-ounce) can corn kernels
1 425-g (15-ounce) can creamed corn
3 cups (420 g) cooked, cubed ham
230 g (8 ounces) shredded cheddar cheese

- Cook potatoes with half chicken stock in saucepan.
- Sauté celery and onion in large soup pot with a little oil.
- Add flour and mix well on medium heat. Add remaining stock and cream. Cook, stirring constantly, until mixture thickens.
- Add potatoes, cayenne pepper, corn, creamed corn, ham, cheese and a little salt and pepper. Heat slowly and stir several times to keep from sticking. Serves 8.

Ham Chowder

This is a really tasty way to use leftover ham. It has a great flavour!

1 cup (100 g) sliced celery
½ cup (80 g) chopped onion
2 tablespoons (30 g) butter
3 cups (210 g) shredded cabbage
3½ cups (490 g) cooked, diced ham
2 425-g (15-ounce) cans stewed tomatoes with liquid
2 teaspoons (10 ml) paprika
1 425-g (15-ounce) can corn kernels, drained
1 425-g (15-ounce) can whole potatoes, drained, sliced
½ litre carton chicken stock
½ cup (135 g) tomato sauce
¼ cup (55 g) lightly packed brown sugar
½ teaspoon garlic powder

- Sauté celery and onion in butter in large roasting pan or soup pot over medium heat.
- Add remaining ingredients plus 1 cup (250 ml) water and ½ teaspoon salt and bring to a boil.
- Reduce heat, cover and simmer for 1 hour. Serves 6 to 8.

Caraway-Potato Chowder

510 g (18 ounces) frozen hash browns
1 onion, chopped
1 red capsicum, seeded, chopped
½ litre carton chicken stock
1 280-g (10-ounce) can cream of celery soup
500 ml (1 pint) unthickened cream
2 teaspoons caraway seeds, crushed
1½ cups (210 g) cooked, chopped ham
½ teaspoon seasoned lemon pepper

- Combine hash browns, onion, capsicum and chicken stock in large saucepan.
- Bring to boil, reduce heat and simmer for 10 to 15 minutes or until potatoes are tender. Do not drain.
- Stir constantly on medium heat and add celery soup, cream, caraway seeds, ham and lemon pepper.
- Heat just until thoroughly hot. Serves 8.

Women are more than twice as likely as men to cite soup as a typical lunch (10 percent versus 4 percent).

Potato-Ham Chowder

This is a great recipe to use when you have leftover ham!

3 medium potatoes
1 litre carton chicken stock
5 tablespoons (70 g) butter
2 sticks celery, chopped
1 onion, chopped
2 280-g (10-ounce) cans cream of celery soup
455 g (16 ounces) frozen corn
1 425-g (15-ounce) can creamed corn
500 ml (1 pint) unthickened cream
3 cups (420 g) cooked, cubed ham

- Peel potatoes, cut in small chunks and cook with half chicken stock in medium saucepan.
- Melt butter in large soup pot and sauté celery and onion.
- Add soup and remaining chicken stock, stir constantly and cook until slightly thick.
- Add cooked potatoes with liquid and remaining ingredients plus 1½ teaspoons salt and ½ teaspoon pepper.
- Heat slowly and stir several times to keep from sticking. Serves 8.

TIP: This will only serve 6 to 8 because everyone will want a second bowl.

Rich Corn Chowder

8 ears fresh corn
8 slices bacon
1 small onion, chopped
½ red capsicum, seeded, chopped
1 small baking potato, peeled, cubed
500 ml (1 pint) unthickened cream
2 teaspoons sugar
½ teaspoon dried thyme
1 tablespoon (15 ml) cornflour

- Cut corn from cobs into large bowl and scrape well to remove all milk.
- Fry bacon in large soup pot over medium heat, remove bacon and save drippings in pan. Crumble bacon and set aside.
- Cook onion and capsicum in drippings until tender.
- Stir in corn, potato, 1 cup (250 ml) water and a little salt and pepper. Bring to boil, cover, reduce heat and simmer for 15 minutes, stirring occasionally.
- Stir in 1½ cups (375 ml) cream, sugar and thyme.
- Combine cornflour and remaining cream and stir until smooth. Gradually add to corn mixture and stir constantly.
- Cook for 15 minutes, stirring constantly until soup thickens. Serves 6.

Veggie-Ham Chowder

1 large onion, chopped
3 sticks celery, sliced
Olive oil
3 cups (210 g) shredded cabbage
3 cups (420 g) cooked, cubed ham
2 425-g (15-ounce) cans stewed tomatoes
1 425-g (15-ounce) can corn kernels, drained
1 425-g (15-ounce) can whole new potatoes, sliced
1 litre carton chicken stock
1 cup (265 g) thick-and-chunky salsa

- Sauté onion and celery in large soup pot with a little oil over medium-high heat.
- Add remaining ingredients, bring to boil, reduce heat and simmer for 30 minutes. Serves 6.

Sausage Chowder

455 g (1 pound) pork sausage
2 425-g (15-ounce) cans kidney beans, rinsed, drained
1 425-g (15-ounce) can diced tomatoes
1 medium potato, peeled, cubed
1 green capsicum, seeded, chopped
1 onion, chopped
1 teaspoon minced garlic
¼ teaspoon thyme

- Brown and cook sausage in large soup pot and drain.
- Add beans, tomatoes, potatoes, capsicum, onion, garlic, thyme and a little salt and pepper.
- Bring to boil, reduce heat and simmer for 1 hour. Serves 6.

Sausage-Bean Chowder

910 g (2 pounds) pork sausage meat
1 425-g (15-ounce) can borlotti beans with liquid
1 425-g (15-ounce) can cannellini beans with liquid
1 425-g (15-ounce) can kidney beans, drained
2 425-g (15-ounce) cans stewed tomatoes
1 litre carton chicken stock
1 teaspoon minced garlic

- Brown and cook sausage in soup pot and stir until sausage crumbles.
- Add all beans, tomatoes, stock and garlic and bring to boil.
- Reduce heat to low and simmer for 20 minutes. Serves 8.

Sausage and Corn Chowder

150 g (⅓ pound) hot Italian sausage
2 310-g (11-ounce) cans corn kernels with liquid
1½ litres chicken stock

- Remove casing from sausage, place in frypan, crumble and cook over medium heat.
- Stir in corn and chicken stock. Mix well and simmer for 10 minutes or until hot. Serves 6.

Green Chilli-Corn Chowder

115 g (¼ pound) bacon
1 medium onion, minced
1 425-g (15-ounce) can corn kernels with liquid
1 425-g (15-ounce) can stewed tomatoes
2–3 fresh green chillies, roasted, peeled, seeded, chopped
2 large baking potatoes, peeled, cubed
1 teaspoon sugar
2 teaspoons paprika
1 145-g (5-ounce) can evaporated milk

- Cut bacon into very small pieces and fry to crisp in frypan.
- Add onion and cook until translucent. Transfer to soup pot.
- Add corn, tomatoes, chillies, potatoes, sugar, ½ teaspoon salt, paprika and 3 cups (750 ml) boiling water.
- Cook on medium-low until potatoes are tender.
- Remove from heat and slowly stir in evaporated milk. Serve immediately. Serves 6 to 8.

Satisfying Seafood Delights

From rich, hearty chowders to Cajun-style seafood gumbos, these seafood specialties are special treats.

Satisfying Seafood Delights Contents

The word 'chowder' comes from the French word 'chaudiere', a cauldron in which fishermen made their stews fresh from the sea. Chowder is a thick, chunky seafood or other thick, rich soup containing chunky food (such as corn chowder). Chowder can contain any of several varieties of seafood and vegetables.

Spiked Crab Soup

30 g (1 ounce) dry onion soup mix
1 170-g (6-ounce) can crabmeat with liquid, flaked
250 ml (8 ounces) pouring cream
½ cup (125 ml) white wine

- Dissolve soup mix with 2 cups (500 ml) water in saucepan.
- Add crabmeat, crab liquid and cream. Season with a little salt and pepper.
- Heat, but do not boil, and simmer for 20 minutes. Stir in wine, heat and serve warm. Serves 6.

Carolina She-Crab Soup

4 cups (1 L) milk
¼ teaspoon nutmeg
1 teaspoon grated lemon peel
455 g (1 pound) fresh crabmeat, flaked
500 ml (1 pint) pouring cream
¼ cup (60 g) butter
½ cup (30 g) cracker crumbs
2 tablespoons (30 ml) sherry

- Pour milk, nutmeg and lemon peel in double boiler and simmer for 5 minutes.
- Add crabmeat, cream and butter and cook over low heat for 15 minutes.
- Stir in cracker crumbs a little at a time to get consistency desired and season soup with a little salt and pepper.
- Cover, remove from heat and set aside for 5 to 10 minutes so flavours blend. Add sherry before serving. Serves 6.

Oyster Soup

1 litre carton chicken stock
1 large onion, chopped
3 sticks celery, sliced
1 red capsicum, seeded, chopped
2 teaspoons minced garlic
2 500-ml (1-pint) cartons fresh oysters, rinsed, drained
½ cup (115 g) butter
¼ cup (60 ml) flour
2 cups (500 ml) milk
1 tablespoon (15 ml) dried parsley

- Combine stock, onion, celery, capsicum and garlic in soup pot. Bring to boil, reduce heat and simmer, stirring occasionally, for 30 minutes.
- Boil oysters in 2 cups (500 ml) water in saucepan for 2 minutes, stirring often or until edges of oysters begin to curl.
- Remove oysters with slotted spoon, coarsely chop half and set aside.
- Pour oyster stock into soup pot with vegetables.
- Melt butter in saucepan over medium heat, gradually whisk in flour and cook for 1 minute.
- Add flour mixture to soup pot and simmer, stirring occasionally over medium heat for 3 minutes.
- Stir in chopped oysters, milk, parsley and a little salt and pepper.
- Cook and stir occasionally over medium heat for 8 minutes or until mixture thickens.
- Stir in remaining whole oysters. Serves 6 to 8.

Seafood Bisque

¼ cup (60 g) butter
230 g (8 ounces) frozen prawns, thawed
1 170-g (6-ounce) can crab, drained, flaked
1 425-g (15-ounce) can whole new potatoes, drained, sliced
1 teaspoon minced garlic
½ cup (60 g) flour
1 litre carton chicken stock
1 cup (250 ml) unthickened cream

- Melt butter in large saucepan on medium heat. Add prawns, crab, new potatoes and garlic and cook for 10 minutes.
- Stir in flour and cook, stirring constantly for 3 minutes.
- Gradually add chicken stock, cook and stir until mixture thickens.
- Stir in cream and a little salt and pepper, stirring constantly and cook just until mixture is thoroughly hot; do not boil. Serves 6.

Cajun Soup

2 tablespoons (30 g) butter
1 onion, chopped
1 red capsicum, seeded, chopped
1 green capsicum, seeded, chopped
2 sticks celery, sliced
1 teaspoon minced garlic
170 g (6 ounces) instant rice
2 425-g (15-ounce) cans stewed tomatoes
1 teaspoon Cajun seasoning
230 g (8 ounces) frozen prawns, thawed

- Melt butter and sauté onions, capsicum, celery and garlic in large frypan.
- Stir in 1 cup (250 ml) water, rice, tomatoes and Cajun seasoning and bring to boil.
- Reduce heat to medium and cook, stirring often, for 6 minutes.
- Add prawns, cover and simmer for additional 5 minutes. Serves 6.

Use frozen vegetables such as peas, spinach or corn to cut prep time. Add them to assorted soups or puree them with stock, cream and sautéed onion, then simmer to make a smooth soup.

Low Country Crab Soup

1 onion, quartered
1 medium leek, white only
1 carrot, scraped, cut into 2.5-cm (1-inch) pieces
3 sticks celery, cut into 2.5-cm (1-inch) pieces
¼ cup (60 g) butter
1 teaspoon minced garlic
¼ cup (30 g) flour
½ litre carton chicken stock
1 L (2 pints) unthickened cream
1 tablespoon (15 ml) mixed herbs
¼ teaspoon cayenne pepper
455 g (1 pound) fresh lump crabmeat, flaked, drained
¼ cup (60 ml) brandy
1 tablespoon (15 ml) chopped fresh parsley

- Puree onion, leek, carrot and celery in blender.
- Melt 2 tablespoons (30 g) butter in soup pot over medium heat, add pureed vegetables and garlic. Cover and cook for 8 minutes, stirring often.
- Stir in flour, cook for 1 minute and stir often.
- Gradually stir in stock, 1 pint (500 ml) cream, herbs, cayenne pepper and a little salt. Cook for 10 minutes and stir occasionally.
- Melt remaining butter in small frypan, add crabmeat, toss gently over medium heat until thoroughly hot; stir in brandy.
- Stir crabmeat mixture, parsley and remaining cream into vegetables in soup pot. Heat until thoroughly hot. Serves 6.

Crab Bisque

1 280-g (10-ounce) can cream of celery soup
1 280-g (10-ounce) can beef, tomato and pepper soup
500 ml (1 pint) light cream
1 170-g (6-ounce) can crabmeat, drained, flaked
⅓ cup (75 ml) sherry

- Mix soups and cream in saucepan.
- Stir in crabmeat and heat through.
- Just before serving, add sherry and stir. Serves 6.

Easy Oyster Stew

3 fresh spring onions, finely chopped
2 tablespoons (30 g) butter
1 340-g (12-ounce) container oysters with liquid
500 ml (1 pint) pouring cream
2 cups (500 ml) milk

- Sauté spring onions in butter in stew pot.
- Add oysters, cream, milk and a little salt and pepper.
- Cook over low heat until oyster edges begin to curl and mixture is hot, but not boiling. Serves 6.

TIP: If you want a little snap to this stew, add cayenne pepper to taste.

Frogmore Stew

Frogmore Stew originated in America in South Carolina's Low Country and dates back many years. According to one story passed down through the years, an old fisherman gathered up whatever he could find to put in a stew. Other stories credit specific people on St. Helena Island with the invention, but there's no disagreement about the fact that Frogmore Stew is a combination of sausage, seafood and corn. Here's one version of the famous American dish.

2 litre cartons fish stock
1.4 kg (3 pounds) smoked sausages, sliced
3 onions, peeled, chopped
1 lemon, sliced, seeded
½ cup (115 g) butter
6 ears corn, halved
1.4 kg (3 pounds) large prawns, peeled

- Combine about 1.5 gallons (6 L) water, stock, sausage, onions, lemon and a little salt and pepper in very large stew pot and bring to boil. Simmer for 45 minutes.
- Add butter and corn and cook for 10 minutes.
- Add prawns, cook for additional 5 minutes and drain water. Serve immediately. Serves 8.

Fresh Oyster Stew

2 500-ml (1-pint) cartons fresh oysters with liquid
3 slices bacon
1 small onion, chopped
2 sticks celery, chopped
1 115-g (4-ounce) can sliced mushrooms
1 280-g (10-ounce) can creamy potato soup
3 cups (750 ml) unthickened cream
⅓ cup (20 g) fresh chopped parsley

- Drain oysters and save liquid.
- Fry bacon in frypan until crisp, drain bacon and crumble. Set aside.
- Cook onion and celery in bacon fat in large frypan on medium heat until tender.
- Add mushrooms, soup, oyster liquid, cream and a little salt and pepper. Heat over medium heat, stirring occasionally, until mixture is thoroughly hot.
- Stir in bacon and oysters and heat for additional 4 to 5 minutes or until edges of oysters begin to curl.
- Sprinkle with parsley. Serves 6 to 8.

Easy New England Clam Chowder

1 cup fish stock
1 175-g (6.5-ounce) can clams, chopped
1 280-g (10-ounce) can cream of celery soup
1 280-g (10-ounce) can creamy potato soup
1 280-g (10-ounce) can French onion soup
1 425-g (15-ounce) can creamed corn
1 cup (250 ml) milk

- Combine all ingredients in saucepan. Heat and stir. Serves 6 to 8.

Clam Chowder Snap

1½ cups fish stock
1 280-g (10-ounce) can cream of celery soup
1 280-g (10-ounce) can creamy potato soup
1 175-g (6.5-ounce) can chopped clams, drained
1 soup can milk

- Combine all ingredients in saucepan. Heat and stir. Serves 6.

Three-Can Clam Chowder

1 cup fish stock
1 175-g (6.5-ounce) can clams, chopped
1 280-g (10-ounce) can cream of celery soup
1 280-g (10-ounce) can creamy potato soup
1 soup can milk

- Combine all ingredients in saucepan and mix well.
- Heat thoroughly and serve. Serves 4.

Cod and Corn Chowder

8 slices bacon
455 g (1 pound) cod, cut into bite-size pieces
2 large baking potatoes, thinly sliced
3 sticks celery, sliced
1 onion, chopped
1 425-g (15-ounce) can corn kernels
250 ml (8 ounces) pouring cream

- Fry bacon in large, heavy soup pot, remove bacon and drain. Crumble bacon and set aside.
- Drain fat from soup pot and stir in 2½ cups (625 ml) water, cod, potatoes, celery, onion, corn and a little salt and pepper. Bring to boil, reduce heat, cover and simmer for about 20 minutes or until fish and potatoes are done.
- Stir in cream and heat just until chowder is thoroughly hot. When serving, sprinkle crumbled bacon over each serving. Serves 6.

Crab-Corn Chowder

60 g (1.8 ounces) dry onion soup mix
2 cups (500 ml) milk
1 230-g (8-ounce) can corn kernels, drained
115 g (4 ounces) cubed cheddar cheese
1 200-g (7-ounce) can crabmeat, flaked

- Combine soup mix and milk in large saucepan, cook over medium heat and stir constantly until soup begins to thicken.
- While still on medium heat, stir in corn and cheese and stir until cheese melts.
- Just before serving, add crabmeat and stir until thoroughly hot. Serves 6.

Oyster and Vegetable Chowder

¼ cup (60 g) butter
3 230-g (8-ounce) cans whole oysters with liquid
455 g (16 ounces) frozen broccoli florets
280 g (10 ounces) frozen corn
500 ml (1 pint) light cream
1 cup (250 ml) milk

- Melt butter in large saucepan and stir in oysters, broccoli and corn. Cook over medium heat and stir often for 12 minutes or until vegetables are tender.
- Stir in cream, milk, 1½ teaspoons salt and ½ teaspoon pepper.
- Cook over low heat and stir often until mixture is thoroughly hot. Serves 6.

Seafood Chowder

3 onions, chopped
2 capsicums, seeded, chopped
2 sticks celery, sliced
¼ cup (60 ml) olive oil
3 tablespoons (20 g) flour
3 425-g (15-ounce) cans stewed tomatoes
1 teaspoon minced garlic
1 teaspoon hot sauce
910 g (2 pounds) medium fresh prawns, peeled
455 g (1 pound) fresh lump crabmeat, flaked
1 340-g (12-ounce) carton oysters, drained

- Sauté onions, capsicums and celery in hot oil in soup pot.
- Add flour and cook for 1 minute, stirring constantly.
- Stir in tomatoes, garlic, hot sauce and a little salt and pepper. Bring to boil, reduce heat and simmer for 15 minutes.
- Add prawns, crabmeat and oysters to soup. Cover and simmer for 15 minutes. Serves 8.

Cauliflower-Crab Chowder

455 g (16 ounces) frozen cauliflower
¼ cup (60 g) butter
¼ cup (30 g) flour
½ litre carton chicken stock
1½ cups (375 ml) milk
85 g (3 ounces) cream cheese, cubed
1 chopped roasted red capsicum
1 teaspoon dried parsley
230 g (8 ounces) refrigerated, imitation crabmeat, drained

- Cook cauliflower in ¾ cup (175 ml) water in large saucepan until tender but crisp.
- In separate saucepan, melt butter, stir in flour and mix well. Add stock, milk and cream cheese and cook, stirring constantly, until thick and bubbly.
- Add mixture to saucepan with cauliflower and stir in roasted red capsicum, parsley and a little salt and pepper.
- Stir in crab and heat just until thoroughly hot. Serves 8.

Everybody's Seafood Gumbo

¼ cup (60 g) butter
¼ cup (30 g) flour
680–910 g (1½–2 pounds) fresh okra, sliced
2 425-g (15-ounce) cans whole tomatoes, chopped
½ cup (80 g) minced onion
455 g (1 pound) prawns, peeled, cleaned
455 g (1 pound) crabmeat, flaked, drained
455 g (1 pound) fish fillets, quartered
1 495-g (1-pint) carton fresh oysters with liquid
Rice, cooked

- Melt butter in heavy frypan and add flour. Stir well over medium heat to make smooth, paste-like roux. When roux is rich brown colour, add a little salt and pepper and mix well.
- Add 2 quarts (2 L) water, okra, tomatoes and onion. Cook on low for 20 minutes.
- Add all seafood and cook on medium-low for 30 minutes or until desired consistency. Serve over rice. Serves 8.

Seafood Gumbo

¼ cup (60 ml) olive oil
½ cup (60 g) flour
1 onion, finely chopped
2 teaspoons minced garlic
2 cups chopped okra
1 425-g (15-ounce) can diced tomatoes
¾ teaspoon cayenne pepper
455 g (1 pound) fresh, peeled, veined prawns
455 g (1 pound) crabmeat, flaked, drained
1 495-g (1-pint) carton oysters, drained
3 fresh spring onions, sliced
Rice, cooked

- Mix oil and flour in large soup pot. Cook over medium heat and stir constantly until paste-like roux turns light brown.
- Add onion, garlic, okra and tomatoes and cook on medium heat for about 10 minutes.
- Stir in 1 cup (250 ml) water, 2 teaspoons salt and cayenne pepper and simmer for 25 minutes.
- Add prawns and crabmeat and simmer for 10 minutes.
- Add oysters and cook for additional 5 minutes.
- Stir in spring onions and serve over rice. Serves 8.

Super Easy Gumbo

1 280-g (10-ounce) can beef, vegetable and pepper soup
1 280-g (10-ounce) can chicken soup
1 170-g (6-ounce) can white crabmeat, flaked
1 170-g (6-ounce) can prawns, cocktail, drained

- Combine all ingredients with 1½ soup cans water in saucepan.
- Cover and simmer for 15 minutes. Serves 4.

Okra Gumbo

455 g (1 pound) fresh okra, sliced
1 onion, chopped
½ cup (115 g) butter
1 large potato, peeled, chopped
2 425-g (15-ounce) cans diced tomato
1 425-g (15-ounce) can corn kernels
Rice, cooked

- Sauté okra and onion in butter in soup pot until light brown on outside.
- Add potato, tomatoes and corn and simmer for about 30 minutes or until okra and potatoes are tender. Serve over rice. Serves 6.

Veggie Meatless Masterpieces

Enjoy a rich, creamy bowl of piping hot cheese soup or maybe a nice bowl loaded with big chunks of potatoes and hearty vegetables. They're wonderful.

Veggie Meatless Masterpieces Contents

Veggie Meatless Masterpieces Contents

If you cook your pasta before adding it to your soup, it doesn't bring all the starch with it and can be added last so it doesn't get overcooked. You can even use leftover pasta that you have stored in the fridge.

The Ultimate Cheddar Cheese Soup

1 cup (160 g) finely chopped onion
1 red capsicum, seeded, diced
2 tablespoons (30 g) butter
455 g (16 ounces) shredded extra sharp cheddar cheese
2 tablespoons (15 g) cornflour
½ litre carton chicken stock
280 g (10 ounces) frozen broccoli florets, thawed
1 170-g (8-ounce) can sliced carrots
1 teaspoon Worcestershire sauce
½ teaspoon garlic powder
500 ml (1 pint) unthickened cream

- Sauté onion and capsicum in butter in large saucepan.
- Mix cheese and cornflour in bowl.
- Pour stock and cheese-cornflour mixture, a little at a time over onion and capsicum and heat, stirring constantly, until cheese melts.
- Stir until smooth and add broccoli, carrots, Worcestershire sauce, ¼ teaspoon (1 ml) each of salt and pepper and garlic powder.
- Simmer and slowly add cream while stirring. Do not boil. Serve immediately. Serves 6.

Old-Time Cheese Soup

¼ cup (60 g) butter
1 small onion, finely chopped
2 sticks celery, finely chopped
½ cup (55 g) shredded carrots
¼ cup (30 g) flour
1 tablespoon (15 ml) cornflour
4 cups (1 L) milk
1 litre carton chicken stock
340 g (12 ounces) cubed cheddar cheese
1 tablespoon (15 ml) dried parsley

- Melt butter in heavy saucepan on medium heat and sauté onion, celery and carrots for about 10 minutes.
- Stir in flour and cornflour and cook on low heat until bubbly.
- Gradually stir in milk and stock and blend into a smooth sauce.
- Add cheese; heat and stir constantly until mixture is smooth.
- Season with a little salt and pepper and stir in parsley. Heat, but do not boil. Serves 8.

The ladies of the French court of Louis XI mostly ate soups and broth because they believed that chewing would cause wrinkles, ruining their facial features.

Country Cheddar Cheese Soup

¼ cup (60 g) butter
2 sticks celery, chopped
1 small onion, finely chopped
1 capsicum, seeded, chopped
1 carrot, peeled, shredded
½ litre carton chicken stock
½ cup (115 g) butter
⅔ cup (80 g) flour
1 quart (1 L) milk
230 g (8 ounces) shredded sharp cheddar cheese

- Melt ¼ cup (60 g) butter and cook celery, onion, capsicum and carrot in saucepan until tender, stirring often.
- Stir in chicken stock, bring to boil, reduce heat and cook on low heat for 10 minutes.
- While vegetables cook, heat ½ cup (115 g) butter in large saucepan, stir in flour and cook, stirring constantly until bubbly.
- Remove from heat and gradually add milk. Cook over medium heat, stirring often, until soup thickens, but do not boil.
- Stir in cheese and heat until cheese melts.
- Stir in vegetable-stock mixture and heat just until hot. Serves 8.

Beer-Cheese Soup

¼ cup (60 g) butter
¼ cup (30 g) flour
500 ml (1 pint) light cream
1 340-g (12-ounce) can beer (not light)
455 g (16 ounces) cubed, cheddar cheese
¼ teaspoon cayenne pepper
2 teaspoons marinade for chicken
Hot sauce

- Melt butter in large soup pot and add flour, stir until smooth and cook for 1 minute.
- Gradually add cream and beer and cook over medium heat, stirring constantly, until thick.
- Add cheese and stir until cheese melts.
- Stir in cayenne pepper, marinade for chicken, a little salt and a dash of hot sauce, if you like. Heat while stirring and ladle into soup bowls. Serves 6.

Incredible Broccoli-Cheese Soup

This really is an incredible soup!

280 g (10 ounces) frozen chopped broccoli
3 tablespoons (40 g) butter
¼ onion, finely chopped
¼ cup (30 g) flour
500 ml (1 pint) unthickened cream
½ litre carton chicken stock
⅛ teaspoon cayenne pepper
230 g (8 ounces) cubed, cheddar cheese

- Punch several holes in broccoli package and microwave for 5 minutes. Turn package in microwave and cook for additional 4 minutes. Leave in microwave for 3 minutes.
- Melt butter in large saucepan and sauté onion, but do not brown.
- Add flour, stir and gradually add cream, chicken stock, ½ teaspoon salt, ⅛ teaspoon pepper and cayenne pepper.
- Stir constantly and heat until mixture is slightly thick. Do not let mixture boil.
- Add cheese, stir constantly and heat until cheese melts.
- Add cooked broccoli. Serve piping hot. Serves 4 to 6.

Creamy Chilli-Cheese Soup

½ onion, minced
1 large tomato, minced
1 large, fresh green chilli, peeled, seeded, minced
½ clove garlic, minced
3 tablespoons (40 g) butter
½ litre carton chicken stock
2 tablespoons (15 g) flour
3 cups (750 ml) milk
340 g (12 ounces) shredded Colby cheese

- Sauté onion, tomato, green chilli and garlic until translucent in large frypan with 1 tablespoon (15 ml) butter.
- Pour in chicken stock, stir gently and pour into large saucepan.
- Melt 2 tablespoons (30 g) butter and add flour to frypan, stir constantly until mixture is smooth and beige in colour. Stir out any lumps.
- Slowly pour in 1½ cups (375 ml) milk and stir constantly until sauce thickens slightly.
- Pour mixture into saucepan and continue cooking on low heat.
- Pour in remaining milk, ½ teaspoon salt, ¼ teaspoon pepper and cheese into saucepan and stir constantly. Simmer until cheese melts.
- Pour into soup cups and serve immediately. Serves 6.

Fiesta Tortilla Soup con Queso

1 litre carton chicken stock
2 425-g (15-ounce) cans stewed tomatoes
4 spring onions with tops, chopped
2 diced green chillies
1 clove garlic, minced
8 corn tortillas
2 tablespoons (30 ml) oil
455 g (16 ounces) cubed cheddar cheese

- Pour chicken stock, tomatoes, onions, green chillies and garlic in large saucepan and heat on medium.
- Cut tortillas into long, narrow strips. Fry tortilla strips with hot oil in frypan for about 10 seconds or until strips are crisp. Remove from frypan and drain.
- Heat soup to boiling, reduce heat to low and stir in cheese.
- Serve in individual bowls and garnish with tortilla strips. Serves 8.

Herbs will have a more intense flavour if they are added when the soup is almost ready to serve.

Best-Ever Cheese Soup

¼ cup (60 g) butter
1 bunch fresh spring onions, sliced
4 sticks celery, sliced
1½ litres chicken stock
2 280-g (10-ounce) cans creamy potato soup
340 g (12 ounces) shredded cheddar cheese
230 g (8 ounces) sour cream

- Melt butter in large soup pot and sauté onions and celery until tender.
- Add stock and bring to a boil, reduce heat and simmer for 20 minutes.
- Stir in potato soup and cheese and heat, stirring constantly until cheese melts. Stir in sour cream and heat, stirring constantly but do not boil. Serves 6 to 8.

Guacamole Soup

1 510-g (18-ounce) can tomato juice
½ cup (80 g) chopped onion
2 avocados, peeled, seeded, diced

- Heat tomato juice and onion in soup pot for 5 minutes or until very hot.
- Stir in three-fourths of diced avocado and heat.
- Sprinkle remaining avocado on top of soup as a garnish and serve immediately. Serves 4.

Cream of Artichoke Soup

2 shallots, finely chopped
2 tablespoons (30 g) butter
2 tablespoons (15 g) flour
½ litre carton chicken stock
1¼ cups (90 g) artichoke hearts, rinsed, drained, chopped
3 tablespoons (10 g) fresh minced parsley
1¼ cups (310 ml) unthickened cream

- Sauté shallots in saucepan with butter until they are transparent.
- Add flour, stir to remove lumps and cook.
- Remove from heat and stir in chicken stock, artichoke hearts and 2 tablespoons (10 g) parsley.
- Return to medium heat and cook for 5 minutes.
- Puree mixture in blender. Strain pureed mixture through coarse sieve and return to clean saucepan.
- Heat on medium, slowly add cream and blend thoroughly.
- Serve hot or cold. Garnish with remaining parsley, if desired. Serves 4.

Asparagus Soup

¼ cup (60 g) butter
1½ litres chicken stock
¾ teaspoon garlic powder
1 bunch spring onions with tops, diced
1 large potato, peeled, cubed
115 g (4 ounces) cubed cheddar cheese
1 425-g (15-ounce) can cut asparagus
230 g (8 ounces) sour cream
Bacon bits

- Combine butter, stock, garlic, spring onion and potato in large saucepan.
- Heat and cook for 15 minutes or until potatoes are tender.
- Add cheese and heat long enough for cheese to melt.
- Stir in asparagus. Fold in sour cream and heat (do not boil) just enough to make soup hot.
- Sprinkle bacon bits over top of each serving. Serves 6 to 8.

Some of the greatest artists in history were inspired by soup: Pablo Picasso painted 'La Soup'; Vincent Van Gogh painted 'Bowls and Bottles'; and James McNeill Whistler painted 'Soupe a Trois Sous'.

Creamy Asparagus Soup

1 onion, finely chopped
1 red capsicum, seeded, chopped
2 tablespoons (30 g) butter
2 425-g (15-ounce) cans cut asparagus, drained
2 280-g (10-ounce) cans cream of chicken soup
500 ml (1 pint) unthickened cream
1 teaspoon lemon juice
¼ teaspoon dried tarragon

- Sauté onion and capsicum in butter in soup pot.
- Add asparagus and blend in food processor until smooth.
- Return onion-asparagus mixture to soup pot and add chicken soup, cream, lemon juice, tarragon and a little salt and pepper.
- Cook on medium-high heat and stir constantly until soup is thoroughly hot. Serves 6.

At-Home Black Bean Soup

2 onions, finely chopped
3 teaspoons minced garlic
Olive oil
4 cups black beans, soaked overnight
1 litre carton beef stock
1½ teaspoons dried cumin
2 teaspoons chilli powder
Shredded sharp cheddar cheese

- Sauté onions and garlic in soup pot with a little oil and cook on medium heat for 5 minutes.
- Place 1 cup beans and about ½ cup (125 ml) stock in food processor and process until beans are smooth.
- Transfer to soup pot and stir in remaining beans, remaining stock, cumin, chilli powder and a little salt and pepper.
- Bring to boil, reduce heat and simmer for 15 minutes.
- Sprinkle cheese over each serving. Serves 4 to 6.

Black Bean Soup

455 g (1 pound) dried black beans
1 litre carton chicken stock
2 onions, chopped
1 capsicum, seeded, chopped
1 tablespoon (15 ml) minced garlic
2 tablespoons (30 ml) olive oil
2 280-g (10-ounce) cans tomatoes
2 chopped green chillies
1 teaspoon chilli powder
⅓ cup (75 ml) lemon juice
230 g (8 ounces) sour cream

- Sort and rinse beans and place in soup pot. Cover with water 5 cm (2 inches) above beans. Bring beans to a boil, cover, remove from heat and let stand for 1 hour. Drain beans and return to soup pot.
- Add chicken stock to beans in pot, cover and cook over medium heat for 3 hours or until beans are tender. Stir occasionally. If beans get a little too dry, add ½ to 1 cup (125 to 250 ml) water.
- Sauté onions, capsicum and garlic in hot oil in large frypan until tender.
- Stir in tomatoes, green chillies, chilli powder, lemon juice and a little salt and pepper and cook for additional 5 minutes.
- Process 2 cups (250 g) cooked beans in food processor until smooth.
- Stir remaining beans into soup pot and add onion-tomato mixture. Cook just until thoroughly hot, ladle into soup bowls and top each bowl with dollop of sour cream. Serves 8.

Ranchero Black Bean Soup

1 cup (125 g) dried black beans
1½ litres beef stock
1 large bunch spring onions with tops, chopped
5 sticks celery, chopped
3 cloves garlic, minced
½ cup (115 g) butter
½ cup (50 g) rice
1 bay leaf
6 peppercorns
½ teaspoon cayenne pepper

- Sort beans, rinse and soak in water overnight. Drain beans, transfer to large saucepan and cook for about 2 hours in beef stock.
- Sauté onions, celery and garlic in butter in frypan until onions are translucent.
- Transfer onions, celery, garlic, rice, bay leaf, peppercorns, 1 teaspoon salt and cayenne pepper to beans.
- Cook for additional 2 hours or until beans are tender. (Add water if needed.)
- Remove bay leaf and peppercorns before serving. Serves 6.

TIP: When serving, it is a nice touch to garnish with shredded cheese, sour cream or chopped spring onions.

Southwestern Bean Soup

Don't let the number of ingredients discourage you. Ask yourself this question, 'Can I open cans?'

¼ cup (60 g) butter
1 onion, chopped
1 capsicum, seeded, chopped
2 teaspoons minced garlic
2 425-g (15-ounce) cans stewed tomatoes
1 425-g (15-ounce) can borlotti beans, drained
1 425-g (15-ounce) can kidney beans, rinsed, drained
1 425-g (15-ounce) can lentils, rinsed, drained
1 tablespoon (15 ml) chilli powder
¼ teaspoon ground coriander
1 cup (115 g) shredded cheddar cheese blend
1 cup (115 g) shredded Colby cheese

- Melt butter in large saucepan on medium heat and cook onion, capsicum and garlic for 5 minutes.
- Stir in tomatoes, lentils and beans, chilli powder, coriander and a little salt and pepper.
- Bring to boil, reduce heat, cover and simmer for 25 minutes.
- Stir in cheddar cheese and cook over low heat, stirring occasionally just until cheese melts.
- Ladle into individual soup bowls and sprinkle Colby cheese over each serving. Serves 8.

Zesty Black Bean Soup

2 onions, finely chopped
Olive oil
3 teaspoons minced garlic
1 tablespoon (15 ml) chilli powder
4 cups black beans, soaked overnight
1 teaspoon ground cumin
½ litre carton beef stock

- Sauté onions in soup pot with a little oil, cook on medium heat for 5 minutes and stir in garlic and chilli powder.
- Puree 1 can beans and add to onion mixture.
- Add remaining beans, cumin and beef stock. Bring to boil, reduce heat and simmer for 10 minutes. If you like, garnish with shredded cheese or salsa just before serving. Serves 6.

Black Bean-Corn Soup

1 onion, chopped
3 teaspoons minced garlic
Olive oil
1 795-g (28-ounce) can diced tomatoes
2 cups black beans, soaked overnight
280 ml (10 ounces) frozen corn
½ cup (85 g) cooked instant rice
1 red capsicum, seeded, chopped
1 teaspoon dried cumin

- Sauté onion and garlic in a little oil in large soup pot for about 5 minutes.
- Stir in tomatoes, beans, corn, rice, capsicum and cumin.
- Cover pot and bring to boil. Reduce heat and simmer for 15 minutes. Serves 6.

Creamy Broccoli Soup

2 tablespoons (30 g) butter
½ cup (80 g) chopped onion
1 280-g (10-ounce) can cream of celery soup
1 cup (250 ml) milk
115 g (4 ounces) cream cheese, cubed
230 g (8 ounces) cubed cheddar cheese
280 g (10 ounces) frozen chopped broccoli florets

- Melt butter in large, heavy soup pot and sauté onion for 5 minutes.
- Stir in soup, milk and cream cheese. Cook on medium-low heat and stir well until cream cheese melts.
- Add cheese, broccoli and a little salt and pepper. Cook on medium-low heat for 10 minutes or until cheese melts and soup is thoroughly hot. Serves 6.

Mexican Bean Soup

1 425-g (15-ounce) can refried beans
1 425-g (15-ounce) can borlotti beans
1 chopped jalapeno chilli
1 230-g (8-ounce) can tomato soup
½ cup (130 g) hot salsa
1 onion, chopped
1 capsicum, seeded, chopped
1 litre carton beef stock

- Combine all ingredients plus 1 cup (250 ml) water and mix well.
- Bring to boil in large soup pot, reduce heat and simmer for 30 minutes. Serves 6.

Chickpea Soup

2 tablespoons (30 ml) olive oil
1 onion, chopped
1 red capsicum, chopped
1 green capsicum, chopped
2 teaspoons minced garlic
½ teaspoon dried sage
1 425-g (15-ounce) can stewed tomatoes
1 litre carton vegetable stock
1 425-g (15-ounce) can chickpeas, drained
½ cup (55 g) elbow macaroni
1 teaspoon Italian seasoning
145 g (5 ounces) grated parmesan cheese

- Combine olive oil, onions, capsicum and garlic in soup pot and cook, stirring often on medium heat for 5 minutes or until onions are translucent.
- Stir in sage, tomatoes, stock, chickpeas and a little salt and pepper and cook for 10 minutes.
- Stir in pasta and Italian seasoning and cook for about 15 minutes or until pasta is al dente (tender, but not overdone).
- Place about 1 heaped tablespoon (15 ml) parmesan cheese over each serving. Serves 6.

Broccoli-Cheddar Soup for Two

⅓ cup (55 g) chopped onion
⅓ cup (35 g) sliced celery
¼ cup (60 g) butter
¼ cup (30 g) flour
½ litre carton chicken stock
1½ cups (375 ml) milk or unthickened cream
280 g (10 ounces) frozen chopped broccoli florets, thawed, cooked
⅔ cup (75 g) shredded cheddar cheese

- Sauté onion and celery in butter in large saucepan.
- Stir in flour and a little salt and pepper. Cook and stir constantly until smooth.
- Add stock and cream and cook, stirring until mixture thickens.
- Add broccoli and simmer, stirring constantly, until mixture is thoroughly hot.
- Remove from heat, add cheese and stir until cheese melts. Serves 2.

In southern Italy, soup is said to relieve your hunger, quench your thirst, fill your stomach, clean your teeth, make you sleep, help you digest and colour your cheeks.

At-Home Broccoli Soup

¼ cup (60 g) butter
2 onions, finely chopped
3 tablespoons (20 g) flour
1½ litres chicken stock
455 g (16 ounces) frozen chopped broccoli florets
1 cup (70 g) shredded carrots
1 145-g (5-ounce) can evaporated milk

- Melt butter in soup pot and sauté onions for 5 to 6 minutes or until golden. Add flour and stir constantly until light brown. Stir in stock and bring to boil, reduce heat and simmer for 10 minutes, stirring constantly.
- Add broccoli and carrots and cook on medium heat for 10 minutes. Stir in evaporated milk and a little salt and pepper. Heat just until soup is thoroughly hot. Serves 6.

Broccoli-Wild Rice Soup

This is a hearty and delicious soup full of flavour.

170 g (6 ounces) chicken-flavoured wild rice mix
280 g (10 ounces) frozen chopped broccoli florets
2 teaspoons dried minced onion
1 280-g (10-ounce) can cream of chicken soup
230 g (8 ounces) cream cheese, cubed

- Combine rice, rice seasoning packet and 6 cups (1.4 L) water in large saucepan. Bring to boil, reduce heat, cover and simmer for 10 minutes, stirring once.
- Stir in broccoli and onion and simmer for 5 minutes.
- Stir in soup and cream cheese. Cook and stir on low heat until cheese melts. Serves 6.

Cheese-Topped Broccoli Soup

1 litre carton chicken stock
2 sticks celery, sliced
1 onion, chopped
1 medium baking potato, peeled, chopped
455 g (16 ounces) frozen chopped broccoli florets
500 ml (1 pint) unthickened cream
145 g (5 ounces) grated parmesan cheese

- Combine stock, celery, onion and chopped potato in large, heavy soup pot.
- Bring to boil, reduce heat and simmer for 20 minutes or until vegetables are tender.
- Stir in broccoli and bring to boil, reduce heat and simmer for 15 minutes. Stir in cream, ¼ teaspoon pepper and a little salt.
- Heat on medium, stirring constantly until soup is thoroughly hot. Ladle into individual soup bowls and sprinkle with parmesan. Serves 6.

Welcome Home Soup

2 cups (140 g) fresh broccoli florets
4–5 large new (red) potatoes, chopped
1 bunch spring onions with tops, chopped
1 litre carton chicken stock
Sour cream

- Cook vegetables in chicken stock until tender and season with a little salt and pepper.
- Pour into blender and puree.
- Pour into soup bowls and garnish with dollop of sour cream. Serves 6 to 8.

Cream of Cauliflower Soup

1 onion, chopped
½ teaspoon garlic powder
Olive oil
1 litre chicken stock
1 large cauliflower, cut into small florets
1½ cups (115 g) pouring cream

- Sauté onion and garlic powder in a little oil.
- Stir in stock and boil. Add cauliflower and cook, stirring occasionally for 15 minutes or until tender.
- Process soup in batches in blender until smooth and return to pan.
- Stir in cream and add a little salt and pepper.
- Cook over low heat, stirring often until thoroughly hot. Serves 6.

Cream of Carrot Soup

1 small onion, chopped
2 tablespoons (30 g) butter
6 carrots, chopped
2 tablespoons (30 ml) dry white wine
1 litre carton chicken stock
⅛ teaspoon ground nutmeg
250 ml (8 ounces) pouring cream, whipped

- Sauté onion in butter and add carrots, wine, chicken stock, nutmeg, ½ teaspoon pepper and a little salt in large saucepan.
- Bring to boil, reduce heat and simmer for 30 minutes or until carrots are tender.
- Pour half of carrot mixture into blender, cover and blend on medium speed until mixture is smooth. Repeat with remaining mixture.
- Return to saucepan and heat just until hot. Stir in cream. Serves 6.

Wine is a great flavour addition to soups and stews. When using wine or alcohol in soup, use less salt because the wine tends to intensify saltiness. Wine should be added at a ratio of no more than ¼ cup wine to 1 quart (litre) soup.

Cauliflower-Potato Soup

1 cup (60 g) instant mashed potato flakes
½ cup (80 g) finely chopped spring onions, white part only
½ teaspoon caraway seeds
1 litre carton chicken stock
455 g (16 ounces) frozen cauliflower florets
230 g (8 ounces) shredded cheddar cheese

- Combine 1½ cups (375 ml) boiling water, dry mashed potatoes, spring onions, caraway seeds, 1½ teaspoons salt, 1 teaspoon pepper and chicken stock in soup pot.
- Bring to boil, reduce heat to medium and simmer for 10 minutes.
- Stir in cauliflower florets and cook for about 10 minutes or until cauliflower is tender.
- Stir in half cheddar cheese and serve in individual soup bowls with couple tablespoons cheese over top of each serving. Serves 8.

Cheesy Cauliflower Soup

455 g (16 ounces) frozen cauliflower florets
2 sticks celery, sliced
1 carrot, peeled, cut into chunks
1 onion, chopped
3 chicken stock cubes
½ teaspoon lemon pepper
250 ml (8 ounces) pouring cream
230 g (8 ounces) shredded Colby cheese

- Combine 2 cups (500 ml) water, cauliflower, celery, carrot, onion, chicken stock cubes, ½ teaspoon salt and lemon pepper in large, heavy soup pot.
- Cover and cook for 1 hour or until vegetables are very tender.
- Pour half mixture into food processor and process until smooth. Repeat with remaining soup mixture.
- Return to soup pot and stir in cream and about three-fourths of cheese.
- Cook over medium heat, stirring constantly until cheese melts and mixture is thoroughly hot.
- Ladle into individual serving bowls and sprinkle remaining cheese over each serving. Serves 6 to 8.

Speedy Cauliflower Soup

1 litre carton chicken stock
1 280-g (10-ounce) can creamy potato soup
1 chopped roasted red capsicum
455 g (16 ounces) frozen cauliflower
500 ml (1 pint) unthickened cream

- Combine stock, potato soup, roasted red capsicum and ¾ cup (175 ml) water in large saucepan.
- Bring to boil, reduce heat and simmer for 10 minutes.
- Stir in cauliflower and cook for additional 20 minutes.
- Add cream and heat just until soup is thoroughly hot. Serves 6.

Quick-and-Easy Corn Soup

2 425-g (15-ounce) cans corn kernels
1 280-g (10-ounce) can creamy potato soup
½ litre carton chicken stock
250 ml (8 ounces) pouring cream
⅛ teaspoon cayenne pepper

- Combine corn, potato soup, stock, cream and cayenne pepper in saucepan.
- Cook on medium heat, stirring often until thoroughly hot. Serves 6.

Corn Soup Olé

2 425-g (15-ounce) cans corn kernels
½ onion, chopped
2 tablespoons (30 g) butter
2 tablespoons (15 g) flour
1 litre carton chicken stock
1½ cups (375 ml) unthickened cream
230 g (8 ounces) shredded cheddar cheese
2 chopped green chillies
Corn chips
Bacon bits

- Sauté corn and onion in butter in soup pot.
- Add flour, ½ teaspoon salt and ¼ teaspoon pepper and cook for 1 minute.
- Gradually add stock and cream while on medium-low heat. Cook and stir until it thickens slightly.
- Add cheddar cheese and green chillies. Heat but do not boil.
- Serve soup in individual bowls and stir in 4 to 5 crumbled corn chips. Garnish with bacon bits. Serves 6.

Creamy Corn Soup

¼ cup (60 g) butter
1 onion, chopped
1 red capsicum, chopped
1 green capsicum, chopped
455 g (16 ounces) frozen corn
1 425-g (15-ounce) can creamed corn
1 280-g (10-ounce) can diced tomatoes
2 chopped green chillies
1 litre carton chicken stock
¼ cup (30 g) flour
500 ml (1 pint) unthickened cream

- Melt butter and sauté onions and capsicums in soup pot on medium heat for 5 minutes.
- Stir in corn, creamed corn, tomatoes, green chillies and chicken stock. Bring to boil, reduce heat and simmer for 20 minutes.
- Mix ¼ cup (60 ml) water with flour in bowl and mix until they blend well. Stir into soup and heat, stirring constantly until soup thickens.
- Stir in cream and heat soup, stirring constantly until thoroughly hot. Serves 8.

Quickie Corny Soup

3 slices bacon
1 small bunch spring onions, minced
1 425-g (15-ounce) can creamed corn
1 280-g (10-ounce) can cream of celery soup
1 soup can filled with milk

- Fry bacon in large frypan and drain. Add onions to frypan and sauté until translucent. Crumble bacon and sprinkle in frypan.
- Add creamed corn, soup, milk and a little salt and pepper. Heat almost to boiling, stir often and pour into soup bowls. Serves 6.

TIP: If you want to add some type of garnish on top of the soup, fry some extra bacon and crumble it over the top or chop the spring onion tops and sprinkle them on top. It looks and tastes great.

Quick Corn Chowder

2 baking potatoes, peeled, diced
½ cup (35 g) shredded carrots
½ cup (80 g) finely chopped onion
1 425-g (15-ounce) can creamed corn
1 230-g (8-ounce) can corn kernels
1 280-g (10-ounce) can cream of celery soup
1 cup (250 ml) milk
230 g (8 ounces) cubed cheddar cheese

- Cook potatoes, carrots and onion in 1½ cups (375 ml) water in large saucepan for about 15 minutes or until potatoes are tender; do not drain.
- Stir in creamed corn, corn, soup, milk and a little salt and pepper. Heat and stir constantly until mixture is thoroughly hot; stir in cheese and serve. Serves 6.

Merry Split Pea Soup

455 g (1 pound) split peas
1 teaspoon dried parsley
½ teaspoon garlic salt
1 litre carton chicken stock
1½ cups (150 g) chopped onion
1¼ cups (150 g) chopped celery
¾ cup (85 g) chopped carrots

- Soak peas overnight in water. Drain, rinse and pour 2 quarts (2 L) water over peas in large soup pot. Add parsley, garlic salt, chicken stock, onion, celery and ¾ teaspoon pepper.
- Cover and simmer for about 1 hour 30 minutes to 2 hours. Add carrots. Cover and simmer for additional 45 minutes. Serves 6.

Mexican-Style Minestrone Soup

455 g (16 ounces) frozen vegetables
1 cup cooked macaroni
1 455-g (16-ounce) jar thick-and-chunky salsa
1 425-g (15-ounce) can borlotti beans with liquid
1 teaspoon chilli powder
1 teaspoon ground cumin
230 g (8 ounces) shredded cheddar cheese

- Combine pasta, vegetables, salsa, beans, chilli powder, cumin and 1 cup (250 ml) water in large saucepan.
- Bring to boil, reduce heat, simmer for about 8 minutes and stir occasionally.
- When ready to serve, top each serving with cheese. Serves 6 to 8.

Minestrone soup comes from the Italian word 'minestra', which means minister. Clergy ministered to the poor by providing bowls of broth containing potatoes, corn, zucchini, tomatoes, capsicums and kidney beans.

Italian Minestrone

1 onion, chopped
1 red capsicum, chopped
1 green capsicum, chopped
3 sticks celery, chopped
2 teaspoons minced garlic
¼ cup (60 g) butter
2 421-g (15-ounce) cans diced tomatoes
1 teaspoon dried oregano
1 teaspoon dried basil
1 litre carton beef stock
2 425-g (15-ounce) cans kidney beans, drained
2 medium zucchini, cut in half lengthwise, sliced
1 cup (105 g) elbow macaroni

- Sauté onions, capsicums, celery and garlic in butter for about 2 minutes in soup pot.
- Add tomatoes, oregano, basil and a little salt and pepper. Bring to boil, reduce heat and simmer for 15 minutes, stirring occasionally.
- Stir in beef stock, beans, zucchini and pasta and bring to boil. Reduce heat and simmer for additional 15 minutes or until pasta is tender. Serves 8.

Minestrone has come to mean 'big soup' and is traditionally a thick Italian vegetable soup that usually contains pasta, beans and sometimes meat, peas and other vegetables. This soup is usually topped liberally with grated parmesan cheese and is hearty enough to be considered a complete meal.

Creamy Mushroom Soup

690 g (32 ounces) fresh mushrooms
1 small onion, finely chopped
¼ cup (60 g) butter, melted
½ cup (60 g) flour
1 litre carton chicken stock
500 ml (1 pint) unthickened cream
250 ml (8 ounces) pouring cream
¼ cup (60 ml) dry white wine
1 teaspoon dried tarragon
2 teaspoons marinade for chicken

- Coarsely chop and sauté mushrooms and onion in butter in large soup pot.
- Add flour and stir until smooth.
- Add stock, cream, pouring cream, wine, tarragon, marinade and about 1 teaspoon (5 ml) salt and stir constantly.
- Bring to boil, reduce heat to medium and cook for 20 minutes or until mixture thickens. Stir often. Serves 6.

Mushroom Soup

1 280-g (10-ounce) can cream of mushroom soup
1 400-g (14-ounce) can sliced mushrooms, drained
½ litre carton beef stock
250 ml (8 ounces) pouring cream

- Combine all ingredients in medium saucepan.
- Mix well and heat thoroughly. Serves 4.

Microwave Mushroom Soup

1 280-g (10-ounce) can cream of mushroom soup
½ litre carton beef stock
1 115-g (4-ounce) can sliced mushrooms, drained

- Combine mushroom soup and stock in 2-L (2-quart) bowl and mix well. Microwave on high for 1 minute and stir.
- Add sliced mushrooms and mix. Reduce heat to medium and microwave for additional 1 minute or until hot.
- Stir before serving. Serves 4.

Lunch-Ready Mushroom Soup

2 tablespoons (30 g) butter
2 tablespoons (15 g) flour
½ litre carton chicken stock
1 cup (250 ml) milk
230 g (8 ounces) fresh mushrooms, sliced
1 teaspoon minced garlic
1 teaspoon dried parsley
1 teaspoon lemon juice
1 cup (250 ml) unthickened cream

- Melt butter, stir in flour in large saucepan and cook, stirring constantly for 1 minute.
- Gradually stir in stock and milk, stirring constantly and bring to a boil.
- Add mushrooms, garlic, parsley, lemon juice and a little salt and pepper and simmer for 5 minutes.
- Add cream and heat just until soup is thoroughly hot, do not boil. Serves 4 to 6.

Favourite Onion Soup

8 onions, thinly sliced
¼ cup (60 g) butter
2 litre cartons beef stock
8 slices bread, crust trimmed, toasted
8 slices Swiss cheese

- Place onions and butter in large soup pot and sauté onions until golden brown. Add beef stock and cook on medium heat for 1 hour.
- Just before time to serve, pour soup into 6 to 8 individual, ovenproof soup bowls, top with slices of toasted bread and cover with slices of cheese.
- Place bowls on baking tray and place under griller for 1 to 2 minutes or until cheese melts. Serve immediately. Serves 6 to 8.

Easy Veggie Soup

1 litre carton beef stock
½ cup (50 g) diced celery
1 455-g (16-ounce) can mixed vegetables
1 bay leaf

- Mix all ingredients in large soup pot.
- Add 1½ cups (375 ml) water, 1 teaspoon each of salt and pepper and simmer for 45 minutes.
- Adjust seasonings, remove bay leaf and serve. Serves 4 to 6.

Tomato-French Onion Soup

1 280-g (10-ounce) can condensed tomato soup
2 280-g (10-ounce) cans French onion soup
Croutons
Grated parmesan cheese

- Combine soups and 2 soup cans water in saucepan. Heat thoroughly.
- Serve in bowls topped with croutons and sprinkle of cheese. Serves 4.

Creamy Parsley Soup

680 g (1½ pounds) zucchini, chopped
1 litre carton chicken stock
2 cups (120 g) loosely packed parsley
250 ml (8 ounces) pouring cream

- Combine zucchini and chicken stock in soup pot and cook until tender.
- Add parsley and cook for additional 5 minutes.
- Process in blender until smooth. Return to soup pot over low heat and slowly stir in cream. Season with a little salt and pepper. Serves 4.

Creamy Green Pea Soup

455 g (16 ounces) frozen green peas
1 cup (250 ml) milk
1 280-g (10-ounce) can cream of chicken soup
½ litre carton chicken stock
1 cup (250 ml) unthickened cream
Shredded Swiss cheese

- Cook peas according to package directions, place peas and milk in blender and blend to uniform consistency.
- Stir in soup, stock, ½ teaspoon pepper and a little salt. Bring to boiling (but do not boil), stirring constantly, reduce heat and simmer for 2 minutes.
- Stir in cream and heat soup just until thoroughly hot. Sprinkle cheese over top of each serving. Serves 6.

Luncheon Pea Soup

1 cup (60 g) instant mashed potato flakes
½ cup (125 ml) Italian salad dressing
455 g (16 ounces) frozen peas
1 litre carton chicken stock
½ cup (120 g) sour cream

- Heat 1¼ cups (310 ml) water in large saucepan, stir in potato flakes and cook for 10 minutes. Stir in salad dressing and peas.
- Transfer soup mixture to blender. Cover and blend small batches until smooth.
- Return blended mixture to saucepan and add chicken stock and ¾ teaspoon pepper. Bring to boil, reduce heat and simmer for about 15 minutes, stirring often.
- Stir in sour cream. Serves 4 to 6.

Quick-and-Easy Peanut Soup

¼ cup (60 ml) butter
1 onion, finely chopped
2 sticks celery, chopped
2 280-g (10-ounce) cans cream of chicken soup
2 soup cans filled with milk
1¼ cups (360 g) crunchy peanut butter

- Melt butter in saucepan and sauté onion and celery over low heat.
- Blend in soups and milk and stir.
- Add peanut butter, stirring constantly and continue to heat until mixture blends well. Serves 4 to 6.

Cream of Peanut Soup

½ cup (115 g) butter
1 onion, finely chopped
1 red capsicum, seeded, chopped
3 sticks celery, finely sliced
¼ cup (30 g) flour
1 litre carton chicken stock
1½ cups (740 g) peanut butter
500 ml unthickened cream
1 cup (250 ml) milk

- Melt butter and sauté onion, capsicum and celery in large saucepan until vegetables are tender.
- Add flour, stir until smooth and cook for 1 minute.
- Gradually add chicken stock, stirring occasionally and cook on low heat for 25 minutes.
- Stir in peanut butter, ½ teaspoon pepper and a little salt.
- Gradually add cream and milk, stir constantly and cook over low heat for 5 minutes or until thoroughly hot. Do not boil. Serves 6.

The ancestor of modern-day stock cubes was 'portable soup' invented in the 18th century. It was made by boiling meat and seasonings until only a thick syrup was left that could be dried and stored for months before being reconstituted.

EZ Potato-Capsicum Soup

510 g (18 ounces) frozen hash browns
1 red capsicum, seeded, chopped
1 litre carton chicken stock
1 280-g (10-ounce) can cream of celery soup
1 280-g (10-ounce) can cream of chicken soup
250 ml (8 ounces) pouring cream
4 fresh spring onions, chopped

- Combine hash browns, capsicum, chicken stock and 1 cup (250 ml) water in large saucepan and bring to a boil.
- Cover, reduce heat and simmer for 25 minutes.
- Stir in both soups and pouring cream and stir well. Cook until thoroughly hot.
- Garnish with spring onions. Serves 6.

TIP: If you like, garnish with shredded cheddar cheese or diced, cooked ham.

Baked Potato Soup

5 large baking potatoes
¾ cup (170 g) butter
⅔ cup (80 g) flour
6 cups (1.4 L) milk
230 g (8 ounces) shredded cheddar cheese
85 g (3 ounces) bacon bits
1 bunch fresh spring onions, chopped
230 g (8 ounces) sour cream

- Cook potatoes in microwave or bake for 1 hour at 205° C (400° F).
- Cut potatoes in half lengthwise, scoop out flesh and save. Discard potato shells.
- Melt butter in large soup pot over low heat, add flour and stir until smooth.
- Gradually add milk and cook over medium heat, stirring constantly, until mixture thickens.
- Stir in potatoes, half cheese, bacon bits, 2 tablespoons (10 g) spring onions and a little salt and pepper. Cook until hot, but do no boil.
- Stir in sour cream and cook just until hot.
- Spoon into soup bowls and sprinkle remaining cheese and spring onions over each serving. Serves 6.

Leek-Potato Soup

910 g (2 pounds) baking potatoes, peeled, cubed
1 litre carton chicken stock
¼ cup (60 ml) butter
3 sticks celery, thinly sliced
¾ cup (70 g) thinly sliced leeks, white only
500 ml unthickened cream
¼ teaspoon ground nutmeg

- Combine potatoes and chicken stock in soup pot. Bring to boil, reduce heat and simmer for 10 to 15 minutes or until potatoes are tender. Do not drain.
- Transfer half potato mixture to blender and blend until smooth. Repeat with remaining potato mixture and return to soup pot.
- Melt butter and cook celery and leeks in saucepan for about 5 minutes or until tender.
- Spoon into soup pot and add cream, nutmeg and a little salt and pepper. Heat, stirring constantly until mixture is thoroughly hot. Serves 6.

In ancient Greece, soup made of peas, lentils and beans was sold in stalls on the street as perhaps the world's first fast food.

Potato-Cheese Soup

4 large potatoes, peeled, cubed
2 carrots, sliced
2 sticks celery, sliced
1 onion, finely grated
¼ cup (60 g) butter
6 chicken stock cubes
¼ teaspoon thyme
½ teaspoon crushed rosemary
¼ teaspoon garlic powder
500 ml cream
1½ cups (170 g) shredded cheddar cheese
3 slices bacon, cooked, crumbled

- Cook potatoes and carrots with enough water to cover vegetables in large saucepan.
- When done, mash with potato masher or mixer, but do not drain water off. Carrots will be chunky.
- Sauté celery and onion in butter in small saucepan and add to mashed potatoes in large saucepan.
- Add all remaining ingredients except bacon and heat just until cheese melts.
- Lower heat, season with a little salt and pepper and simmer for 10 minutes.
- Serve with bacon pieces sprinkled over individual bowls of soup. Serves 6.

Garlic-Potato Soup

4 cups (1 L) milk
200 g (7 ounces) instant mashed potatoes
1 280-g (10-ounce) can cream of celery soup
230 g (8 ounces) shredded sharp cheddar cheese
1 chopped roasted red capsicum

- Combine milk and 3 cups (750 ml) water in soup pot and bring to a boil. Remove from heat, add instant potato mix and stir with whisk until they mix well. Stir in celery soup and mix well.
- Stir in half cheese, roasted red capsicum and ½ teaspoon pepper and stir until cheese melts. Ladle into individual bowls and sprinkle remaining cheese on top of each serving. Serves 6.

Easy Potato Soup

510 g (18 ounces) frozen hash browns
1 cup (160 g) chopped onion
½ litre carton chicken stock
1 280-g (10-ounce) can cream of celery soup
1 280-g (10-ounce) can cream of chicken soup
2 cups (500 ml) milk

- Combine hash browns, onion and 2 cups (500 ml) water in large saucepan and bring to boil.
- Cover, reduce heat and simmer for 30 minutes.
- Stir in stock, soups and milk and heat thoroughly. Serves 8.

Pumpkin Soup

230 g (8 ounces) fresh mushrooms, sliced
3 tablespoons (40 g) butter
¼ cup (30 g) flour
1 litre carton vegetable stock
2 cups cooked pumpkin
500 ml unthickened cream
2 tablespoons (45 g) honey
2 tablespoons (25 g) sugar
½ teaspoon curry powder
¼ teaspoon ground nutmeg

- Sauté mushrooms in butter in large saucepan.
- Add flour, stir well and gradually add stock. Boil and cook for 2 minutes or until mixture thickens.
- Stir in pumpkin, cream, honey, sugar, curry powder and nutmeg.
- Stir constantly until soup is thoroughly hot. Serves 6.

TIP: If you have some sour cream, a dollop of sour cream on top of soup is a very nice garnish.

Spinach Soup

2 280-g (10-ounce) packets frozen chopped spinach, cooked
2 280-g (10-ounce) cans cream of mushroom soup
1 cup (250 ml) unthickened cream
1 litre carton chicken stock

- Puree spinach, mushroom soup and cream in blender in batches.
- Place spinach mixture and chicken stock in saucepan and heat on medium until thoroughly hot.
- Reduce heat to low and simmer for 10 minutes. Serve hot or cold. Serves 6.

Quick Spinach-Rice Soup

1½ litres chicken stock
680 g (24 ounces) frozen spinach, thawed
1 280-g (10-ounce) can cream of onion soup
1 chopped roasted red capsicum
½ cup (50 g) instant rice

- Combine stock, spinach, soup, roasted red capsicum, rice and a little salt and pepper in soup pot.
- Bring to boil, reduce heat and simmer for 10 minutes. Serves 6.

Zesty Squash Soup

2 tablespoons (30 g) butter
1 onion, finely chopped
2 tablespoons (15 g) flour
4 cups yellow squash, chopped
1 litre carton chicken stock
2 chopped green chillies
¾ cup (175 ml) pouring cream

- Melt butter and sauté onion in large soup pot for 3 minutes, stirring constantly.
- Stir in flour and cook for 1 minute.
- Add yellow squash, stock, ½ cup (125 ml) water, green chillies and a little salt and pepper. Bring to boil, reduce heat and simmer for 25 minutes.
- Puree soup in batches in blender until mixture is smooth.
- Return pureed soup to pot, add cream and heat just until soup is thoroughly hot. Serves 6 to 8.

Johnny Appleseed's Pumpkin Soup

1 small butternut pumpkin
3 tart green apples
1 medium onion, chopped
¼ teaspoon dried rosemary
¼ teaspoon dried marjoram
1½ litres chicken stock
2 slices white bread
¼ cup (60 ml) pouring cream

- Cut butternut pumpkin in half and scoop out seeds.
- Peel, core and chop apples.
- Combine all ingredients except cream in large saucepan. Bring to boil, reduce heat and simmer for 45 minutes.
- Remove butternut pumpkin, scoop out flesh from peel and discard peel.
- Add flesh back to mixture and puree in blender until smooth.
- Return mixture to saucepan and bring to boil. Just before serving, mix in cream. Serves 6.

TIP: By adding a bit more cream, this soup also tastes great cold.

Reduced-salt, reduced-fat chicken stock works just as well as chicken stock and helps lower one's sodium intake.

Creamy Butternut Soup

4 cups (450 g) cooked, mashed butternut pumpkin
1 litre carton chicken stock
½ teaspoon sugar
250 ml (8 ounces) pouring cream
¼ teaspoon ground nutmeg

- Combine mashed pumpkin, stock, sugar and a little salt in saucepan. Boil and gradually stir in half of cream. Cook until thoroughly hot.
- Beat remaining cream. When ready to serve, place dollop of whipped cream on soup and sprinkle with nutmeg. Serves 4.

TIP: It takes about 3 to 4 butternut pumpkins to yield 4 cups (450 g).

Cream of Zucchini Soup

455 g (1 pound) fresh zucchini, grated
1 onion, chopped
½ litre carton chicken stock
½ teaspoon sweet basil
500 ml unthickened cream

- Combine zucchini, onion, stock, basil and a little salt and pepper in saucepan.
- Bring to a boil and simmer until soft. Place in food processor and puree.
- Gradually add ½ cup (155 g) cream and blend.
- Return zucchini mixture to saucepan and add remaining cream. Heat, but do not boil. Serves 4 to 6.

Zesty Zucchini Soup

¼ cup (60 g) butter
3 cups (370 g) coarsely chopped zucchini
2 sticks celery, thinly sliced
1½ teaspoons Italian seasoning
½–1 teaspoon curry powder
1 280-g (10-ounce) can creamy potato soup
1 280-g (10-ounce) can French onion soup
2 cups (500 ml) milk

- Melt butter in soup pot and cook on medium-low heat.
- Add zucchini, celery, Italian seasoning and curry powder and stir constantly for 5 minutes.
- Stir in potato soup, onion soup and milk. Bring to boil, reduce heat and simmer for about 10 minutes. Serves 6.

TIP: *If you want to serve with a nice garnish, place croutons and chopped spring onions on top.*

Emma Ewing wrote Soups and Soup Making, *a pamphlet published in 1882. She wrote that soup is 'convenient, economic and healthful'.*

Homemade Tomato Soup

3 425-g (15-ounce) cans whole tomatoes with liquid
½ litre carton chicken stock
1 tablespoon (15 ml) sugar
1 tablespoon (15 ml) minced garlic
1 tablespoon (15 ml) balsamic vinegar
¾ cup (175 ml) pouring cream

- Puree tomatoes in batches with blender and pour into large saucepan.
- Add chicken stock, sugar, garlic, balsamic vinegar and a little salt. Bring to a boil, reduce heat and simmer for 15 minutes.
- Pour in cream, stir constantly and heat until soup is thoroughly hot. Serves 4.

TIP: If you want to fry some bacon or have some ready-cooked, crumbled bacon in the pantry, it would be great as a garnish. If you don't have time, don't worry about it. No one will miss it, if you don't use it.

Creamy Tomato Soup

¼ cup (60 g) butter
1 onion, chopped
2 795-g (28-ounce) cans diced tomatoes with liquid, drained
2 tablespoons (30 g) light brown sugar
2 tablespoons (35 g) tomato paste
2 tablespoons (15 g) flour
½ litre carton chicken stock
250 ml (8 ounces) pouring cream

- Melt butter in large soup pot, sauté onions for about 4 minutes and stir constantly.
- Add drained tomatoes, brown sugar and mixture of tomato paste and flour. Cook, stirring often on medium heat for 10 minutes.
- Gradually stir in stock and reserved tomato juice and simmer on low for 15 minutes.
- Puree soup in batches in food processor until mixture is smooth.
- Pour pureed mixture back into soup pot and heat to boiling.
- Immediately remove from heat. Stir in cream and a little salt. Serves 6.

TIP: If you want a 'snappy' soup with a little fire, just add some hot sauce or a little cayenne pepper. That will get their attention.

Tomato-Basil Soup

2 280-g (10-ounce) cans tomato soup
1 425-g (15-ounce) can diced tomatoes
2 teaspoons finely minced onion
2½ cups (625 g) buttermilk
2 tablespoons (5 g) chopped fresh basil

- Combine tomato soup, tomatoes, onion, buttermilk, basil and ¼ teaspoon pepper and a little salt in saucepan.
- Cook, stirring often for 8 minutes or until thoroughly hot. Serves 4.

Tomato-Ravioli Soup

1 425-g (15-ounce) can stewed tomatoes
1 litre carton chicken stock
¾ teaspoon dried Italian seasoning
340 g (12 ounces) refrigerated cheese-filled pasta
2 small zucchini, sliced
4 fresh spring onions, sliced

- Combine tomatoes, chicken stock, ½ teaspoon pepper and Italian seasoning in large saucepan. Bring to boil, reduce heat and simmer for 5 minutes.
- Add pasta and zucchini and bring to boil, reduce heat and simmer for 8 to 10 minutes or until pasta is tender.
- Sprinkle a few sliced spring onions over each individual serving. Serves 6.

Warm-Your-Soul Soup

1½ litres chicken stock
1 280-g (10-ounce) can Italian-stewed tomatoes with liquid
½ cup (80 g) chopped onion
¾ cup (75 g) chopped celery
170 g (16 ounces) fettuccini (egg noodles)

- Combine chicken stock, tomatoes, onion and celery in large soup pot.
- Bring to boil and simmer until onion and celery are almost done.
- Add pasta and cook al dente (firm but tender). Season with a little salt and pepper. Serves 4 to 6.

Fiesta Soup

1 425-g (15-ounce) can stewed tomatoes
1 teaspoon paprika
1 425-g (15-ounce) can corn kernels
1 425-g (15-ounce) can borlotti beans with liquid
1 litre carton chicken stock
1 280-g (10-ounce) can cream of celery soup

- Combine tomatoes, corn, beans, stock and a little salt and mix well.
- Stir in soup and heat until thoroughly hot. Serves 6.

TIP: *If you want a heartier soup, just add 1 cup of cooked chicken chunks.*

Zippy Tomato Soup

2 tablespoons (30 g) butter
1 onion, chopped
2 sticks celery, sliced
1 capsicum, seeded, chopped
1 teaspoon minced garlic
2 425-g (15-ounce) cans Italian stewed tomatoes
½ litre carton vegetable stock
½ teaspoon cayenne pepper
⅓ cup (80 g) sour cream

- Melt butter in large saucepan and cook onion, celery, capsicum and garlic over medium heat for 10 minutes or until vegetables are tender, but not brown.
- Stir in stewed tomatoes and transfer, in batches, to food processor. Process until soup is almost smooth.
- Return soup mixture to saucepan and add vegetable stock, cayenne pepper and a little salt and pepper.
- Heat for 5 minutes or until soup is thoroughly hot. Stir in sour cream just before serving. Serves 4.

TIP: If you have some croutons in the pantry, throw a couple on top of each soup bowl before you serve. It's a nice touch, but not a 'must-do'.

Tomato-Tortilla Soup

8 corn tortillas, cut into strips
Olive oil
1 onion, chopped
½ cup (75 g) finely chopped green capsicum
½ teaspoon ground cumin
2 teaspoons minced garlic
2 425-g (15-ounce) cans diced tomatoes
2 chopped green chillies
1½ litres chicken stock
½ bunch fresh coriander, very finely chopped
230 g (8 ounces) shredded cheddar cheese

- Fry tortilla strips in hot oil in frypan and drain on paper towels.
- Sauté onion, capsicum, cumin and garlic in 2 tablespoons (30 ml) oil in large heavy soup pot.
- Add diced tomatoes, green chillies, chicken stock and coriander and stir occasionally. Cook on medium heat for 20 to 25 minutes.
- When ready to serve, place some tortilla strips and shredded cheese in each bowl, pour soup into bowls and serve immediately. Serves 4 to 6.

TIP: If you want to make this a hearty, one-dish meal, add 2 cups (280 g) cooked, chopped chicken breasts.

El Paso Tomato Soup

2 280-g (10-ounce) cans tomato soup
2 teaspoons paprika
1 onion, sliced, cooked
2 280-g (10-ounce) cans tomatoes
½ litre carton chicken stock

- Mix all ingredients plus 1 soup can water in saucepan.
- Heat to boiling and stir often. Reduce heat and simmer for 5 minutes. Serves 4.

Spicy Tomato Soup

2 280-g (10-ounce) cans tomato soup
1 425-g (15-ounce) can stewed tomatoes
1 teaspoon chilli powder
2 chopped green chillies
1 280-g (10-ounce) can French onion soup
3 slices bacon, fried, drained, crumbled

- Combine tomato soup, stewed tomatoes, green chillies and onion soup in saucepan and heat thoroughly.
- To serve, sprinkle crumbled bacon on top. Serves 6.

Cheesy Vegetable Soup

2 large potatoes, peeled, diced
1 onion, chopped
1 red capsicum, chopped
1 green capsicum, chopped
1 litre carton chicken stock
1 115-g (4-ounce) can sliced mushrooms, drained
455 g (16 ounces) frozen mixed vegetables
1 280-g (10-ounce) can cream of celery soup
340 g (12 ounces) cubed cheddar cheese

- Combine potatoes, onions, capsicum, chicken stock and 2 cups (500 ml) water in large soup pot on medium heat.
- Cook for 15 to 20 minutes or until potatoes are tender.
- Stir in mushrooms, mixed vegetables and 1 teaspoon salt and cook for additional 10 minutes.
- Stir in celery soup and cheese, heat on medium-low and stir until cheese melts. Serves 6.

Swiss-Vegetable Soup

30 g (1 ounce) vegetable soup mix
1 cup (250 ml) unthickened cream
1½ cups (160 g) shredded Swiss cheese

- Combine soup mix and 3 cups (750 ml) water in saucepan and bring to boil.
- Lower heat and simmer for about 10 minutes.
- Add cream and cheese, stir and serve hot. Serves 4.

Winter Sweet Potato Soup

2 tablespoons (30 g) butter
1 cup (160 g) sliced spring onions, white part only
3 cups cooked sweet potatoes
1 litre carton chicken stock
¼ teaspoon ground cinnamon
½ cup (125 ml) light cream

- Melt butter in large saucepan and sauté spring onions for about 5 minutes.
- Mash sweet potatoes slightly with fork and place in saucepan with onions.
- Add chicken stock, cinnamon and a little salt. Bring to boil, reduce heat and simmer for 5 minutes.
- Stir in cream. Soup may be served warm or chilled. Serves 4.

Southwest Chilli and Tomatoes

4 spring onions, sliced
4 teaspoons minced garlic
2 teaspoons olive oil
2 425-g (15-ounce) cans diced tomatoes with liquid
1 425-g (15-ounce) can borlotti beans, rinsed, drained
¾ teaspoon cayenne pepper
2 tablespoons (15 g) chilli powder
1 teaspoon ground cumin
½ teaspoon coriander
6 fresh sage leaves, snipped

- Sauté spring onions and garlic with olive oil in large saucepan over medium heat for about 3 minutes.
- Add tomatoes, beans, cayenne pepper, chilli powder, cumin, coriander and a little salt.
- Heat chilli to boiling, reduce heat, add sage and cook for 2 minutes.
- Remove sage leaves before serving. Serves 4.

Favourite Veggie-Lovers' Chilli

2 onions, coarsely chopped
2 tablespoons (30 ml) olive oil
2 425-g (15-ounce) cans diced tomatoes
⅔ cup (175 g) medium-hot salsa
2 teaspoons ground cumin
½ teaspoon dried oregano
2 425-g (15-ounce) cans borlotti beans
1 green capsicum, seeded, coarsely chopped
1 red capsicum, seeded, coarsely chopped
1 cup (135 g) halved baby carrots
4 cups (380 g) hot cooked rice
230 g (8 ounces) shredded cheddar cheese

- Sauté onion in oil in large soup pot.
- Add ½ cup (125 ml) water, tomatoes, salsa, cumin, oregano and a little salt and pepper.
- Bring to boil, reduce heat and simmer for 10 minutes.
- Stir in beans, capsicums and carrots. Cover and cook over medium heat for 25 minutes and stir occasionally.
- Spoon rice into individual soup bowls and ladle chilli over rice.
- Sprinkle generous amount of cheddar cheese on top of soup. Serves 6.

Vegetarian Chilli

2 425-g (15-ounce) cans stewed tomatoes
1 425-g (15-ounce) can kidney beans, rinsed, drained
1 425-g (15-ounce) can borlotti beans with liquid
1 onion, chopped
1 green bell pepper, seeded, chopped
1 tablespoon (15 ml) chilli powder
340 g (12 ounces) elbow macaroni
¼ cup (60 g) butter, sliced

- Combine tomatoes, kidney beans, borlotti beans, onion, capsicum, chilli powder and 1 cup (250 ml) water in soup pot. Cover and cook on medium heat for 1 hour.
- Cook pasta according to package directions, drain and add butter. Stir until butter melts.
- Add pasta to chilli and mix well. Serves 6.

Supper-Ready Vegetable Chilli

1 795-g (28-ounce) can diced tomatoes
1 455-g (16-ounce) jar thick-and-chunky salsa
1 cup black beans, soaked overnight
1 425-g (15-ounce) can borlotti beans, drained
1 230-g (8-ounce) can corn kernels
1 tablespoon (15 ml) chilli powder
230 g (8 ounces) shredded cheddar cheese

- Combine tomatoes, salsa, black beans, borlotti beans, corn and chilli powder in large soup pot.
- Bring to boil, reduce heat and simmer for 15 minutes and stir often.
- Before serving, sprinkle 2 to 3 tablespoons (15 to 20 g) cheese over top of each serving. Serves 6.

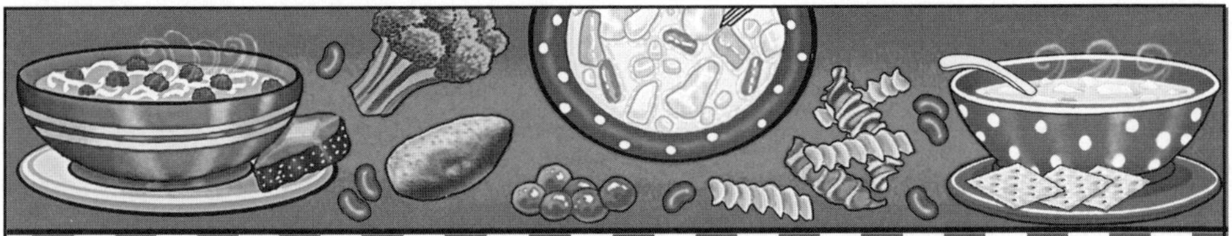

Slow Cooker Soups & Stews

Soup, stew, chilli and chowder recipes for your slow cooker so you can come home to great taste.

Slow Cooker Soups & Stews Contents

Slow Cooker Soups & Stews Contents

An old Yiddish saying affirms what we already know: 'Troubles are easier to take with soup than without'.

Tasty Chicken and Rice Soup

455 g (1 pound) boneless, skinless chicken breast halves
½ cup (95 g) brown rice
1 280-g (10-ounce) can cream of chicken soup
1 280-g (10-ounce) can cream of celery soup
½ litre carton chicken stock
455 g (16 ounces) frozen, sliced carrots, thawed
1 cup (250 ml) unthickened cream

- Cut chicken into 2.5-cm (1-inch) pieces. Place pieces in sprayed 4 to 5-L (4 or 5-quart) slow cooker.
- Mix rice, both soups, chicken stock and carrots in saucepan, heat just enough to mix well and pour over chicken.
- Cover and cook on low for 7 to 8 hours.
- Turn heat to high, add cream and cook for additional 15 to 20 minutes. Serves 6.

A team of scientists at the University of Nebraska confirms what grandmothers have known for centuries – that chicken soup is good for colds. Chicken soup contains several anti-inflammatory ingredients that affect the immune system in a positive way.

Chicken and Rice Soup

170 g (6 ounces) long grain-wild rice mix
30 g (1 ounce) chicken-noodle soup mix
2 280-g (10-ounce) cans cream of chicken soup
2 sticks celery, chopped
2 cups (280 g) cooked, cubed chicken

- Combine all ingredients and about 6 cups (1.4 L) water in 5 to 6-L (5 to 6-quart) slow cooker. Stir soup to mix.
- Cover and cook on low for 2 to 3 hours. Serves 6.

Chicken and Barley Soup

680–910 g (1½–2 pounds) boneless, skinless chicken thighs
455 g (16 ounces) frozen stew vegetables
30 g (1 ounce) vegetable soup mix
1¼ cups (250 g) pearl barley
1 litre carton chicken stock

- Combine all ingredients plus 1 teaspoon each of salt and pepper and 4 cups (1 L) water in large, sprayed slow cooker.
- Cover and cook on low for 5 to 6 hours or on high for 3 hours. Serves 6.

Confetti Chicken Soup

455 g (1 pound) boneless, skinless chicken thighs
170 g (6 ounces) chicken-flavoured rice
1½ litres chicken stock
3 carrots, peeled, sliced
1 280-g (10-ounce) can cream of chicken soup
1½ tablespoons (20 g) chicken seasoning
280 g (10 ounces) frozen corn, thawed
280 g (10 ounces) frozen baby green peas, thawed

- Cut thighs in thin strips.
- Combine chicken, rice, chicken stock, carrots, soup, chicken seasoning and 1 cup (250 ml) water in 5 to 6-L (5 to 6-quart) slow cooker.
- Cover and cook on low for 8 to 9 hours.
- About 30 minutes before serving, turn heat to high and add corn and peas to cooker.
- Continue cooking for additional 30 minutes. Serves 6.

Country Chicken Chowder

680 g (1½ pounds) boneless, skinless chicken breast halves
2 tablespoons (30 g) butter
2 280-g (10-ounce) cans creamy potato soup
½ litre carton chicken stock
280 g (10 ounces) frozen corn
1 onion, sliced
2 sticks celery, sliced
280 g (10 ounces) frozen peas and carrots, thawed
½ teaspoon dried thyme leaves
½ cup (125 ml) unthickened cream

- Cut chicken into 2.5-cm (1-inch) strips.
- Brown chicken strips in butter in frypan and transfer to large sprayed slow cooker.
- Add soup, stock, corn, onion, celery, peas and carrots and thyme to saucepan and heat just enough to mix well. Pour into cooker.
- Cover and cook on low for 3 to 4 hours or until vegetables are tender.
- Turn off heat, stir in cream and set aside for about 10 minutes before serving. Serves 4 to 6.

Chicken-Pasta Soup

680 g (1½ pounds) boneless, skinless chicken thighs, cubed
1 onion, chopped
3 carrots, peeled, sliced
½ cup (65 g) halved pitted black olives
1 teaspoon minced garlic
1½ litres chicken stock
1 425-g (15-ounce) can Italian stewed tomatoes
1 teaspoon Italian seasoning
½ cup (40 g) small shell pasta
Parmesan cheese

- Combine all ingredients, except shell pasta and parmesan cheese in saucepan and heat just enough to mix well. Pour into sprayed slow cooker.
- Cover and cook on low for 8 to 9 hours.
- About 30 minutes before serving, add pasta and stir.
- Increase heat to high and cook for additional 20 to 30 minutes. Garnish with parmesan cheese. Serves 6.

Slow cookers work best when filled to between two-thirds and three-fourths of capacity.

Tortellini Soup

30 g (1 ounce) white sauce mix
3 boneless, skinless chicken breast halves
½ litre carton chicken stock
1 teaspoon minced garlic
½ teaspoon dried basil
½ teaspoon dried oregano
½ teaspoon cayenne pepper
230 g (8 ounces) cheese-filled tortellini
1½ cups (375 ml) unthickened cream
280 g (10 ounces) fresh baby spinach

- Place white sauce mix in sprayed 5 to 6-L (5 to 6-quart) slow cooker. Add 4 cups (1 L) water and stir until mixture is smooth.
- Cut chicken into 2.5-cm (1-inch) pieces.
- Add chicken, stock, garlic, ½ teaspoon salt, basil, oregano and cayenne pepper to white sauce mixture.
- Cover and cook on low for 6 to 7 hours or on high for 3 hours.
- Stir in tortellini, cover and cook 1 hour more on high.
- Stir in cream and fresh spinach and cook just enough for soup to get hot. Serves 6.

Creamy Chicken Soup

2 cups (500 ml) milk
200 g (7 ounces) creamy vegetable instant soup starter
1 cup (140 g) cooked, finely chopped chicken breasts
280 g (10 ounces) frozen green peas, thawed
Shredded cheddar cheese

- Place 5 cups (1.2 L) water and milk in slow cooker. Set heat on high until water and milk come to a boil.
- Stir contents of soup starter into hot water and milk and stir well.
- Add chopped chicken, green peas and a little salt and pepper.
- Cook on low for 2 to 3 hours.
- To serve, sprinkle cheddar cheese over each serving of soup. Serves 4.

Chicken Stew

4 large boneless, skinless chicken breasts, cubed
3 medium potatoes, peeled, cubed
1 740-g (26-ounce) jar meatless spaghetti sauce
1 425-g (15-ounce) can cut green beans, drained
1 425-g (15-ounce) can corn kernels, drained
1 tablespoon (15 ml) mixed herbs

- Combine cubed chicken, potatoes, spaghetti sauce, green beans, corn, mixed herbs and ¾ cup (175 ml) water in 5 to 6-L (5 to 6-quart) slow cooker.
- Cover and cook on low for 6 to 7 hours. Serves 8.

Chicken Stew over Rice

60 g (2 ounces) chicken gravy mix
2 cups (200 g) sliced celery
280 g (10 ounces) frozen sliced carrots, thawed
280 g (10 ounces) frozen green peas, thawed
1 teaspoon dried basil
3 cups (420 g) cooked, cubed chicken or turkey breasts
Rice, cooked

- Combine gravy mix, 2 cups (500 ml) water, celery, carrots, peas, basil, cubed chicken and ¾ teaspoon each of salt and pepper in slow cooker.
- Cover and cook on low for 6 to 7 hours.
- Serve over cooked rice. Serves 6 to 8.

TIP: If you like thick stew, mix 2 tablespoons (15 g) cornflour with ¼ cup (60 ml) water and stir into chicken mixture. Cook for additional 30 minutes to thicken.

Chicken-Tortellini Stew

255 g (9 ounces) cheese-filled tortellini
2 small yellow squash, halved, sliced
1 red capsicum, seeded, chopped
1 onion, chopped
1 litre carton chicken stock
1 teaspoon dried rosemary
½ teaspoon dried basil
2 cups (280 g) cooked, chopped chicken

- Place tortellini, squash, capsicum and onion in slow cooker. Stir in stock, rosemary, basil and chicken.
- Cover and cook on low for 2 to 4 hours or until pasta and vegetables are tender. Serves 6 to 8.

Celery-Chicken Chowder

3 cups (420 g) cooked, cubed chicken
½ litre carton chicken stock
2 280-g (10-ounce) cans creamy potato soup
1 large onion, chopped
3 sticks celery, sliced diagonally
455 g (16 ounces) frozen corn, thawed
⅔ cup (150 ml) pouring cream

- Combine chicken, stock, potato soup, onion, celery, corn and ¾ cup (175 ml) water in 5 to 6-L (5 to 6-quart) slow cooker. Cover and cook on low for 3 to 4 hours.
- Add cream to slow cooker and heat for additional 15 minutes or until thoroughly hot. Serves 6.

Creamy Dreamy Turkey Soup

230 g (8 ounces) fresh mushrooms
2–3 cups (280–420 g) chopped cooked turkey breast
1 large onion, minced
6–8 baby carrots, diced
2 280-g (10-ounce) cans cream of chicken soup
½ cup (125 ml) chicken stock
1 200-g (7-ounce) can green peas, drained
1 diced roasted red capsicum
½ cup (125 ml) milk

- Clean mushrooms, remove stems and make 4 slices of each mushroom. Transfer to sprayed slow cooker.
- Add turkey, onion, carrots, soup and chicken stock and mix well.
- Cook on low for 7 to 8 hours or on high for 3 to 4 hours.
- Add peas, roasted red capsicum and milk and stir well. Cook on low for additional 30 minutes or high for 15 minutes. Serves 8.

Here's a great idea for serving a hearty soup: slice the top off a big, chunky round loaf of bread, hollow out the middle, lightly toast the loaf and fill it with soup for an edible bowl (and easy clean-up). Toast the top and set it beside the bread bowl.

Turkey-Tortilla Soup

1 litre carton chicken stock
2 425-g (15-ounce) cans stewed tomatoes
1 280-g (10-ounce) can butter beans
1 280-g (10-ounce) corn kernels, drained
2 teaspoons chilli powder
1 teaspoon dried coriander
2 cups (110 g) crushed corn chips
2½ cups (350 g) chopped cooked turkey

- Combine stock, tomatoes, butter beans, corn, chilli powder, coriander, ⅓ cup (20 g) crushed corn chips and turkey in large slow cooker and stir well.
- Cover and cook on low for 3 to 5 hours.
- When ready to serve, sprinkle remaining chips over each serving. Serves 6.

TIP: Smoked turkey is just not as good as roasted turkey for this soup.

Turkey-Tortellini-Tomato Soup

455 g (16 ounces) turkey sausage
2 425-g (15-ounce) cans Italian stewed tomatoes
½ litre carton chicken stock
2 280-g (10-ounce) cans French onion soup
1 cup shredded white cabbage
1 cup shredded red cabbage
1 cup shredded carrot
255 g (9 ounces) refrigerated cheese-filled tortellini

- Brown and crumble turkey sausage in frypan, drain and place in large, sprayed slow cooker.
- Add tomatoes, chicken stock, onion soup, cabbage, carrots and 2 cups (500 ml) water.
- Cover and cook on low heat for 5 to 6 hours.
- Turn heat to high and add pasta. Cover and cook for additional 20 minutes. Serves 6 to 8.

Andy Warhol said he painted soup cans because he had soup for lunch every day for 20 years.

Turkey-Mushroom Soup

Here's another great way to use leftover chicken or turkey.

2 cups (145 g) sliced shitake mushrooms
2 sticks celery, sliced
1 small onion, chopped
2 tablespoons (30 g) butter
1 425-g (15-ounce) can sliced carrots, drained
1 litre carton chicken stock
½ cup (40 g) risoni pasta
2 cups (280 g) cooked, chopped turkey (do not use smoked turkey)

- Sauté mushrooms, celery and onion in butter in frypan.
- Transfer to slow cooker and add carrots, stock, risoni and turkey.
- Cover and cook on low for 2 to 3 hours or on high for 1 to 2 hours. Serves 6.

TIP: Button mushrooms are fine for this recipe, too.

Do not use meats that are still frozen in slow cookers as they may not cook thoroughly. However, it is not a problem with frozen vegetables.

Turkey-Veggie Chilli

455 g (1 pound) minced turkey
Olive oil
2 425-g (15-ounce) cans borlotti beans with liquid
1 425-g (15-ounce) can cannellini beans with liquid
½ litre carton chicken stock
2 425-g (15-ounce) cans stewed tomatoes
1 230-g (8-ounce) can corn kernels, drained
1 onion, chopped
1 red capsicum, chopped
1 green capsicum, chopped
2 teaspoons minced garlic
2 teaspoons ground cumin
½ cup (55 g) elbow macaroni

- Cook and brown turkey in frypan with a little oil and place in large slow cooker.
- Add beans, stocks, tomatoes, corn, onions, capsicums, garlic, cumin and a little salt and stir well.
- Cover and cook on low for 4 to 5 hours.
- Stir in pasta and continue cooking for about 15 minutes.
- Stir to make sure pasta does not stick to cooker and cook for additional 15 minutes or until pasta is tender. Serves 8.

TIP: If you want to get 'fancy', top each serving with a dab of sour cream or 1 tablespoon (15 ml) shredded cheddar cheese.

Beef and Barley Soup

455 g (1 pound) lean minced beef
1½ litres beef stcok
¾ cup (150 g) quick-cooking barley
1 onion, chopped
1 red capsicum, chopped
1 green capsicum, chopped
3 cups (365 g) sliced carrots
2 cups (200 g) sliced celery

- Brown beef in frypan, drain and transfer to 5-L (5-quart) slow cooker.
- Add beef stock, barley, onions, capsicums, carrots and celery.
- Cover and cook on low for 7 to 8 hours. Serves 4 to 6.

Beef-Black Bean Soup

455 g (1 pound) lean minced beef
2 onions, chopped
2 cups (200 g) sliced celery
1 litre carton beef stock
1 425-g (15-ounce) can stewed tomatoes
1 teaspoon paprika
3 cups black beans, soaked overnight

- Brown beef in frypan until no longer pink. Place in sprayed 5 to 6-L (5 to 6-quart) slow cooker.
- Add onions, celery, stock, tomatoes, black beans, ¾ cup (175 ml) water and a little salt and pepper.
- Cover and cook on low for 6 to 7 hours or on high for 3 hours 30 minutes. Serves 6.

TIP: If you like zestier soup, add 1 teaspoon (5 ml) chilli powder.

Tasty Cabbage and Beef Soup

455 g (1 pound) lean minced beef
1 cup shredded white cabbage
1 cup shredded red cabbage
1 cup shredded carrot
1 425-g (15-ounce) can cut green beans
1 425-g (15-ounce) can corn kernels
2 425-g (15-ounce) cans Italian stewed tomatoes
1 litre carton beef stock
Cornbread

- Brown beef in frypan, drain fat and place in large slow cooker.
- Add cabbage, carrot, green beans, corn, tomatoes and beef stock and a little salt and pepper.
- Cover and cook on low for 7 to 8 hours. Serve with cornbread. Serves 6.

Saucy Cabbage Soup

455 g (1 pound) lean minced beef
1 small head cabbage, chopped
2 425-g (15-ounce) cans borlotti beans with liquid
1 425-g (15-ounce) can tomato soup
1 425-g (15-ounce) can stewed tomatoes
2 teaspoons chilli powder
½ litre carton beef stock
2 teaspoons ground cumin

- Brown beef in frypan, drain and place in sprayed 5 to 6-L (5 to 6-quart) slow cooker.
- Add cabbage, beans, tomato soup, tomatoes, chilli powder, stock, cumin and 1 cup (250 ml) water and mix well.
- Cover and cook on low for 5 to 6 hours or until cabbage is tender. Serves 6.

Chilli Soup

3 425-g (15-ounce) cans chilli with beans
1 425-g (15-ounce) can corn kernels
½ litre carton beef stock
2 425-g (15-ounce) cans stewed tomatoes
2 teaspoons ground cumin
4 teaspoons chilli powder
Flour tortillas

- Combine chilli, corn, stock, tomatoes, cumin, chilli powder and 1 cup (250 ml) water in 5 to 6-L (5 to 6-quart) slow cooker.
- Cover and cook on low for 4 to 5 hours. Serve with warm, buttered flour tortillas. Serves 6.

Beef-Noodle Soup

680 g (1½ pounds) lean minced beef
1 onion, chopped
2 425-g (15-ounce) cans mixed vegetables
2 425-g (15-ounce) cans Italian stewed tomatoes
1 litre carton beef stock
1 teaspoon dried oregano
280 g (10 ounces) fettuccini (medium egg noodles)

- Brown and cook beef until no longer pink in frypan and transfer to slow cooker.
- Add onion, mixed vegetables, stewed tomatoes, beef stock and oregano. Cover and cook on low for 4 to 5 hours.
- Cook pasta according to package directions. Add pasta to slow cooker and cook for 20 minutes. Serves 6.

Enchilada Soup

455 g (1 pound) lean minced beef, browned, drained
1 425-g (15-ounce) can stewed tomatoes
1 425-g (15-ounce) can borlotti beans with liquid
1 425-g (15-ounce) can corn kernels with liquid
1 onion, chopped
2 280-g (10-ounce) cans enchilada sauce
230 g (8 ounces) shredded cheese
Corn chips

- Combine beef, tomatoes, beans, corn, onion, enchilada sauce and 1 cup (250 ml) water in sprayed 5 to 6-L (5 to 6-quart) slow cooker and mix well.
- Cover and cook on low for 6 to 8 hours or on high for 3 to 4 hours.
- Stir in shredded cheese. If desired, top each serving with a few crushed corn chips. Serves 6.

Keep lid on the slow cooker (unless recipe calls for stirring). The slow cooker can take as long as 20 minutes to regain the heat lost when the cover is removed. Do not cook without cover in place.

Mexican Meatball Soup

1½ litres beef stock
1 455-g (16-ounce) jar hot salsa
455 g (16 ounces) frozen corn, thawed
510 g (18 ounces) frozen meatballs, thawed
1 teaspoon minced garlic

- Combine all ingredients in slow cooker and stir well.
- Cover and cook on low for 4 to 7 hours. Serves 4 to 6.

Beefy Rice Soup

455 g (1 pound) lean beef stew meat
½ litre carton beef stock
200 g (7 ounces) beef-flavoured rice
280 g (10 ounces) frozen peas and carrots
2½ cups (625 ml) tomato juice

- Sprinkle stew meat with pepper, brown in non-stick frypan, drain and place in large slow cooker.
- Add stock, rice, peas and carrots, tomato juice and 2 cups (500 ml) water.
- Cover and cook on low for 6 to 7 hours. Serves 6.

Meatball-Potato Soup

910 g (32 ounces) frozen meatballs, thawed
2 425-g (15-ounce) cans stewed tomatoes
3 large potatoes, peeled, diced
4 carrots, peeled, sliced
2 medium onions, chopped
1 litre carton beef stock
2 tablespoons cornflour

- Combine meatballs, tomatoes, potatoes, carrots, onions, beef stock, a little salt and pepper and 1 cup (250 ml) water in sprayed 6-L (6-quart) slow cooker.
- Cover and cook on low for 5 to 6 hours.
- Turn heat to high. Combine cornflour with ¼ cup (60 ml) water, pour into cooker and stir to mix well.
- Cook for additional 10 or 15 minutes or until slightly thick. Serves 8.

Slow cookers meld flavours deliciously, but colours can fade over long cooking times. You can 'dress up' your dish with colourful garnishes such as fresh parsley or chives, purchased salsa, extra shredded cheeses, and a sprinkle of paprika or a dollop of sour cream.

Taco Soup Olé

910 g (2 pounds) lean minced beef
2 425-g (15-ounce) cans baked beans
1 425-g (15-ounce) can corn kernels, drained
3 425-g (15-ounce) cans stewed tomatoes
2 chopped green chillies
10 g (0.4 ounce) French onion soup mix
30 g (1 ounce) taco seasoning mix

- Brown beef in large frypan, drain and transfer to slow cooker.
- Add 1 cup (250 ml) water and remaining ingredients and stir well.
- Cover and cook on low for 8 to 10 hours. Serves 8.

TIP: *If you have some shredded cheddar cheese, it's fun to sprinkle some over each serving.*

If you need to thicken your soup just add a little pasta or mashed potato flakes.

Taco Soup

680 g (1½ pounds) lean minced beef
1 onion, chopped
30 g (1 ounce) taco seasoning mix
425 g (15 ounces) can corn kernels with liquid
1 425-g (15-ounce) can borlotti beans with liquid
1 425-g (15-ounce) can stewed tomatoes with liquid
½ litre carton beef stcok
Corn chips

- Combine beef and onion in large frypan, brown and drain. Transfer to slow cooker.
- Add taco seasoning, corn, beans, tomatoes, 1 cup (250 ml) water and stock and stir well.
- Cook on low for 3 to 4 hours. Serve with corn chips. Serves 6.

TIP: If you want a garnish, top each serving with a dollop of sour cream. If you don't want to wait 3 to 4 hours, put ingredients in a large soup pot. Bring to boil, reduce heat and simmer for 1 to 2 hours.

Camp Stew in Slow Cooker

455 g (1 pound) lean minced beef
1 onion, chopped
2 large potatoes, peeled, diced
1 425-g (15-ounce) can borlotti beans
1 425-g (15-ounce) can creamed corn
1 230-g (8-ounce) can corn kernels, drained
2 cups cooked chicken
2 425-g (15-ounce) cans stewed tomatoes
1 cup (270 g) tomato sauce
2 tablespoons (30 ml) lemon juice
1 tablespoon (15 ml) Worcestershire sauce
1 teaspoon hot sauce

- Brown and cook beef and onion in large frypan over medium heat and stir until beef crumbles and is no longer pink; drain.
- Layer potatoes, borlotti beans, cooked beef, creamed corn and remaining ingredients in 6-L (6-quart) slow cooker.
- Cover and cook on low for 8 hours or until potatoes are tender. Serves 8.

Hamburger Soup

910 g (2 pounds) lean minced beef
2 425-g (15-ounce) cans chilli
455 g (16 ounces) frozen mixed vegetables, thawed
1½ litres beef stock
2 425-g (15-ounce) cans stewed tomatoes

- Brown beef until no longer pink in frypan and place in 6-L (6-quart) slow cooker.
- Add chilli, vegetables, stock, tomatoes, 1 cup (250 ml) water and 1 teaspoon salt and stir well.
- Cover and cook on low for 6 to 7 hours. Serves 6 to 8.

Meatball-Veggie Stew

510 g (18 ounces) frozen meatballs, thawed
455 g (16 ounces) frozen stew vegetables
1 425-g (15-ounce) can stewed tomatoes
1 340-g (12-ounce) jar beef gravy
2 teaspoons crushed dried basil

- Place meatballs and vegetables in 4 to 5-L (4 to 5-quart) slow cooker.
- Stir stewed tomatoes, gravy, basil, ½ teaspoon pepper and ½ cup (125 ml) water in bowl and mix well.
- Transfer to slow cooker. Cover and cook on low for 6 to 7 hours. Serves 6.

Taco-Chilli Soup

910 g (2 pounds) very lean stew meat
2 425-g (15-ounce) cans stewed tomatoes
30 g (1 ounce) taco seasoning mix
2 425-g (15-ounce) cans borlotti beans with liquid
425 g (15 ounces) can corn kernels with liquid

- Cut large pieces of stew meat in half and brown in large frypan.
- Combine stew meat, tomatoes, chilli powder, taco seasoning, beans, corn and 1½ cups (375 ml) water in 4 to 5-L (4 or 5-quart) slow cooker.
- Cover and cook on low for 5 to 7 hours. Serves 8.

TIP: If you are not into 'spicy', omit the chilli powder.

Hearty Meatball Stew

910 g (32 ounces) frozen meatballs, thawed
2 425-g (15-ounce) cans Italian stewed tomatoes
1 litre carton beef stock
2 425-g (15-ounce) cans new potatoes, drained
455 g (16 ounces) baby carrots
1 tablespoon (15 ml) steak seasoning

- Place meatballs, stewed tomatoes, beef stock, potatoes, carrots and steak seasoning in 6-L (6-quart) slow cooker.
- Cover and cook on low for 6 to 7 hours. Serves 8.

Comfort Stew

680 g (1½ pounds) premium stew meat
2 280-g (10-ounce) cans French onion soup
1 280-g (10-ounce) can cream of onion soup
1 280-g (10-ounce) can cream of celery soup
455 g (16 ounces) frozen stew vegetables, thawed

- Place stew meat in sprayed slow cooker.
- Combine all soups and mix well. Spread evenly over meat, but do not stir.
- Turn slow cooker to high and cook just long enough for ingredients to get hot, about 15 minutes.
- Change heat setting to low, cover and cook for 7 hours.
- Add vegetables and cook for additional 1 hour. Serves 6 to 8.

Canned soups are unquestionably a convenience, and they can often be improved by adding fresh ingredients such as fresh vegetables, meat, spices or even leftovers.

Gringo Stew Pot

680–910 g (1½–2 pounds) lean beef stew meat
2 425-g (15-ounce) cans borlotti beans with liquid
1 onion, chopped
3 carrots, sliced
2 medium potatoes, peeled, cubed
30 g (1 ounce) taco seasoning mix
2 425-g (15-ounce) cans stewed tomatoes
2 teaspoons chilli powder

- Brown stew meat in non-stick frypan.
- Combine meat, borlotti beans, onion, carrots, potatoes, taco seasoning and 2 cups (500 ml) water in large slow cooker.
- Cover and cook on low for 6 to 7 hours.
- Add stewed tomatoes and chilli powder and cook for additional 1 hour. Serves 6.

TIP: This is great served with warmed and buttered flour tortillas.

The one thing a slow cooker will not do is brown the meat; therefore, many recipes suggest browning the meat before placing in cooker.

South-of-the-Border Beef Stew

680–910 g (1½–2 pounds) boneless, beef chuck roast
1 green capsicum, seeded
2 onions, coarsely chopped
2 425-g (15-ounce) cans borlotti beans with liquid
½ cup (50 g) rice
½ litre carton beef stock
2 425-g (15-ounce) cans stewed tomatoes
1 cup (265 g) mild or medium green salsa
2 teaspoons ground cumin
Flour tortillas

- Trim beef and cut into 2.5-cm (1-inch) cubes.
- Brown beef in large frypan and transfer to large sprayed slow cooker.
- Cut capsicum into 1.2-cm (½-inch) slices.
- Add remaining ingredients with a little salt and 1½ cups (375 ml) water to slow cooker.
- Cover and cook on low for 7 to 8 hours.
- Serve with warm flour tortillas. Serves 8.

A Different Stew

910 g (2 pounds) premium-cut stew meat
455 g (16 ounces) frozen Oriental stir-fry vegetables, thawed
1 280-g (10-ounce) can mushroom soup
½ litre carton beef stock
⅔ cup (180 g) bottled sweet-and-sour sauce
1 tablespoon (15 ml) steak seasoning

- Sprinkle stew meat with ½ teaspoon pepper, brown in frypan and transfer to slow cooker.
- Combine vegetables, soup, stock, sweet-and-sour sauce, steak seasoning and 1 cup (250 ml) water in bowl. Pour over stew meat and stir well.
- Cover and cook on low for 7 to 8 hours. Serves 8.

Roast and Vegetable Stew

3 cups (280 g) roast beef, cooked, cubed
2 425-g (15-ounce) cans stewed tomatoes
455 g (16 ounces) frozen mixed vegetables, thawed
1 litre carton beef stock

- Combine all ingredients in 6-L (6-quart) slow cooker with a little salt and pepper. Cover and cook on low for 5 to 7 hours. Serves 6.

TIP: If you want some crunchy vegetables in your soup, add 1 cup (100 g) cauliflower florets and 1 cup (70 g) broccoli florets about 1 hour before serving.

Hungarian Stew

910 g (2 pounds) boneless short ribs
1 cup (200 g) pearl barley
1 small onion, chopped
1 green capsicum, seeded, chopped
1 teaspoon minced garlic
2 425-g (15-ounce) cans kidney beans, drained
1 litre carton beef stock
1 tablespoon (15 ml) paprika

- Combine all ingredients plus 1 cup (250 ml) water in slow cooker.
- Cover and cook on low for 8 to 9 hours or on high for 4 hours 30 minutes to 5 hours. Serves 6.

Easy Chilli

1.8 kg (4 pounds) lean minced beef
60 g (2 ounces) hot chilli mix
1 170-g (6-ounce) can tomato soup
2 425-g (15-ounce) cans stewed tomatoes with liquid
2½ teaspoons ground cumin

- Break beef into pieces, brown in large frypan and drain. Use slotted spoon to drain fat and place beef in 5 to 6-L (5 to 6-quart) slow cooker.
- Add chilli mix, tomato sauce, stewed tomatoes, cumin, 1 teaspoon salt and 1 cup (250 ml) water.
- Cover and cook on low setting for 4 to 5 hours. Serves 6.

TIP: If you think chilli has to have beans, add 2 (15-ounce/425-g) cans baked beans.

Chilli Tonight

910 g (2 pounds) lean coarsely minced beef
1 large onion, finely chopped
1 280-g (10-ounce) can chopped tomatoes
2 chopped green chillies
2½ cups (625 ml) tomato juice
2 tablespoons (15 g) chilli powder
1 tablespoon (15 ml) ground cumin
1 tablespoon (15 ml) minced garlic

- Brown meat in frypan, drain and transfer to large slow cooker.
- Combine minced beef, onion, tomatoes, green chillies, tomato juice, chilli powder, cumin, garlic and 1 cup (250 ml) water and mix well.
- Cover and cook on low for 7 to 8 hours. Serves 6.

Chunky Chilli

910 g (2 pounds) premium-cut stew meat
1 onion, chopped
2 425-g (15-ounce) cans diced tomatoes
2 425-g (15-ounce) cans borlotti beans with liquid
1½ tablespoons (22 ml) chilli powder
2 teaspoons ground cumin
1 teaspoon oregano
Shredded cheddar cheese

- If stew meat is in fairly large chunks, cut each chunk in half. Brown in large frypan and transfer to large slow cooker.
- Add onion, tomatoes, beans, seasonings and a little salt.
- Cover and cook on low for 6 to 7 hours.
- Sprinkle shredded cheddar cheese over each serving. Serves 6.

Black Bean-Chilli Soup

1 litre carton chicken stock
3 cups black beans, soaked overnight
2 280-g (10-ounce) cans tomatoes
2 chopped green chillies
1 onion, chopped
1 teaspoon ground cumin
½ teaspoon dried thyme
½ teaspoon dried oregano
1 tablespoon (15 ml) minced garlic
2–3 cups (280–420 g) cooked, finely diced ham

- Combine chicken stock and black beans in slow cooker and cook on high just long enough for ingredients to get hot.
- With potato masher, mash about half of beans in cooker.
- Reduce heat to low and add tomatoes, green chillies, onion, cumin, thyme, oregano, garlic, ham and ¾ cup (175 ml) water.
- Cover and cook for 5 to 6 hours. Serves 6.

Southern Soup

1½ cups (185 g) dry black-eyed peas
2–3 cups (280–420 g) cooked, cubed ham
1 425-g (15-ounce) can corn kernels, drained
1 cup cut okra
1 onion, chopped
1 large potato, peeled, cubed
2 teaspoons Cajun seasoning
1 litre carton chicken stock
2 425-g (15-ounce) cans stewed tomatoes
2 teaspoons chilli powder

- Rinse peas and drain.
- Combine peas and 5 cups (1.2 L) water in large saucepan. Bring to boil, reduce heat and simmer for about 10 minutes.
- Drain peas and pour into 5 to 6-L (5 to 6-quart) slow cooker.
- Add ham, corn, okra, onion, potato, seasoning, stock and 1 cup (250 ml) water to slow cooker, cover and cook on low for 6 to 8 hours.
- Add stewed tomatoes and chilli powder and continue cooking for additional 1 hour. Serves 6.

Black-Eyed Pea Soup

5 slices thick-cut bacon, diced
1 onion, chopped
1 green capsicum, seeded, chopped
3 sticks celery, sliced
3 cups black-eyed peas, soaked overnight
2 425-g (15-ounce) cans stewed tomatoes with liquid
1 teaspoon chicken seasoning

- Cook bacon pieces until crisp in frypan, drain on paper towel and drop in slow cooker.
- With bacon drippings in frypan, sauté onion and capsicum, but do not brown.
- Transfer onions and capsicum to slow cooker.
- Add celery, black-eyed peas, stewed tomatoes, 3 cups (750 ml) water, 1 teaspoon salt and chicken seasoning.
- Cover and cook on low for 3 to 4 hours. Serves 6.

When cooking soups or stews, leave at least a 5-cm (2-inch) space between the top of the slow cooker and the food so that the mixture can come to a simmer.

Cannellini Bean-Bacon Soup

8 slices thick-cut bacon, divided
1 carrot, halved lengthwise, sliced
3 425-g (15-ounce) cans cannellini beans with liquid
3 sticks celery, chopped
1 onion, chopped
1 litre carton chicken stock
1 teaspoon Italian herb seasoning
1 280-g (10-ounce) can cream of chicken soup

- Cook bacon in frypan, drain and crumble.
- Combine half of crumbled bacon, carrot, beans, celery, onion, stock, seasoning and 1 cup (250 ml) water in 5 to 6-L (5 to 6-quart) slow cooker.
- Cover and cook on low for 5 to 6 hours.
- Ladle 2 cups (500 ml) soup mixture into blender and process until smooth.
- Return to cooker, add soup and stir to mix. Cook on high for additional 10 to 15 minutes.
- Sprinkle remaining bacon crumbles on top of soup before serving. Serves 6.

Ham and Bean Soup

1 onion, finely chopped
2 sticks celery, chopped
2 teaspoons minced garlic
1 litre carton chicken stock
2 425-g (15-ounce) cans baked beans with ham sauce
3 cups (420 g) cooked, cubed ham
⅓ cup (25 g) pasta shells

- Combine onion, celery, garlic, chicken stock, beans, ham and 1 cup (250 ml) water in 5 to 6-L (5 to 6-quart) slow cooker.
- Cover and cook on low for 4 to 5 hours.
- Turn cooker to high heat, add pasta and cook for additional 35 to 45 minutes or until pasta is tender. Serves 6.

TIP: If you have time to fry some bacon, it's great crumbled on top of soup as a garnish.

Always save a ham bone for soups, stews and beans. If you don't need it immediately, just freeze it for later.

Cajun Bean Soup

570 g (20 ounces) soup mix
1 tablespoon (20 ml) Cajun seasoning
2 cups (280 g) cooked, finely chopped ham
1 onion, chopped
2 425-g (15-ounce) cans stewed tomatoes
Cornbread

- Soak beans overnight in large slow cooker.
- After soaking, drain water and cover with 5 cm (2 inches) water over beans.
- Cover and cook on low for 5 to 6 hours or until beans are tender.
- Add ham, onion, stewed tomatoes and seasoning in soup mix.
- Cook on high for 30 to 45 minutes. Serve with cornbread. Serves 6.

Slow-Cook Cannellini Bean Soup

Better than Grandma's!

1½ cups (395 g) dried cannellini beans
1 capsicum, seeded, chopped
1 carrot, finely chopped
2 celery sticks, finely chopped
1 small onion, finely chopped
455 g (1 pound) ham hock

- Soak beans for 8 to 12 hours and drain.
- Place all ingredients in 2-L (2-quart) slow cooker, add 5 cups (1.2 L) water and ½ teaspoon salt and a little pepper.
- Cook for 8 to 10 hours on low setting.
- Remove ham hock and discard skin, fat and bone.
- Cut meat in small pieces and place in soup. Beans can be mashed, if desired. Serves 4 to 6.

Pork and Chickpea Soup

910 g (2 pounds) pork shoulder, cubed
1 onion, chopped
2 sticks celery, sliced
2 425-g (15-ounce) cans chickpeas with liquid
2 425-g (15-ounce) cans stewed tomatoes
1 litre carton chicken stock
1 tablespoon (15 ml) ground cumin
Tortillas
Shredded cheese
Spring onions, chopped

- Sprinkle pork cubes with a little salt and pepper and brown in frypan. Place in 5 to 6-L (5 to 6-quart) slow cooker.
- Combine onion, celery, chickpeas, stewed tomatoes, stock and cumin and pour over pork.
- Cover and cook on high for 6 to 7 hours.
- Serve with warmed, buttered tortillas and top each bowl of soup with some shredded cheese and spring onions. Serves 6.

Slow cooking retains most of the moisture in food; therefore, if a recipe results in too much liquid at the end of the cooking time, remove cover, increase heat to high and cook another 45 minutes.

Winter Minestrone

455 g (1 pound) Italian sausages, sliced
2 medium potatoes, peeled, cubed
2 medium fennel bulbs, trimmed, chopped
2½ cups (600 ml) peeled, chopped butternut pumpkin
1 onion, chopped
1 425-g (15-ounce) can kidney beans, rinsed, drained
2 teaspoons minced garlic
1 teaspoon Italian seasoning
1 litre carton chicken stock
1 cup (250 ml) dry white wine
280 g (10 ounces) fresh spinach, stems removed

- Cook sausage until brown in frypan and drain.
- Combine potatoes, fennel, pumpkin, onion, beans, garlic and Italian seasoning in large slow cooker.
- Top with sausage and pour chicken stock and wine over all.
- Cover and cook on low for 7 to 9 hours.
- Stir in spinach, cover and cook for additional 10 minutes. Serves 8.

Tater Talk Soup

5 medium potatoes, peeled, cubed
2 cups (280 g) cooked, cubed ham
1 cup (70 g) chopped, fresh broccoli florets
1 280-g (10-ounce) can cream of celery soup
1 280-g (10-ounce) can cream of onion soup
½ litre carton chicken stock
2½ soup cans filled with milk

- Place potatoes, ham and broccoli in sprayed slow cooker.
- Combine soups, stock and milk in saucepan and heat just enough to mix until smooth. Pour ingredients in slow cooker. Cover and cook on low for 7 to 8 hours. Serves 8.

Potato Soup

3 large potatoes, peeled, cubed
¼ cup (60 g) butter, sliced
½ litre carton chicken stock
1 onion, finely chopped
2 cups (500 ml) milk
2 cups (280 g) cooked, cubed ham
230 g (8 ounces) cubed cheddar cheese
1 teaspoon dried parsley
250 ml (8 ounces) pouring cream

- Place potatoes, butter, stock, onion, milk and 2 cups (500 ml) water in sprayed 6-L (6-quart) slow cooker.
- Cook on high for 30 minutes, reduce heat to low, cover and cook for 6 to 7 hours.
- Stir in ham, cheese, parsley and a little salt and pepper and cook on high for 20 minutes or until cheese melts. Stir in cream and serve hot. Serves 6.

Spicy Sausage Soup

455 g (1 pound) mild bulk sausage meat
455 g (1 pound) hot bulk sausage meat
2 425-g (15-ounce) cans stewed tomatoes
3 cups (305 g) chopped celery
1 230-g (8-ounce) can sliced carrots, drained
1 425-g (15-ounce) can cut green beans, drained
½ litre carton chicken stock

- Combine mild and hot sausage, shape into small balls and place in non-stick frypan.
- Brown thoroughly, drain and place in large slow cooker.
- Add remaining ingredients with 1 teaspoon salt and 1 cup (250 ml) water to slow cooker and stir gently so meatballs will not break up.
- Cover and cook on low for 6 to 7 hours. Serves 6.

Potato-Leek Soup

30 g (1 ounce) white sauce mix
795 g (28 ounces) frozen hash browns, thawed
3 medium leeks, sliced
3 cups (420 g) cooked, cubed ham
1 340-g (12-ounce) can evaporated milk
230 g (8 ounces) sour cream

- Combine 3 cups (750 ml) water and white sauce in 4 to 5-L (4 to 5-quart) slow cooker and stir until smooth.
- Add hash browns, leeks, ham and evaporated milk. Cover and cook on low for 7 to 9 hours or on high for 3 to 4 hours.
- When ready to serve, turn heat to high and stir in sour cream. Cover and continue cooking for 15 minutes or until mixture is thoroughly hot. Serves 8.

Most slow cooker users suggest 'tasting' before serving to check if any seasonings such as salt, pepper, lemon juice, herb blends or Worcestershire sauce need to be added.

Spicy Black Bean Soup

455 g (1 pound) hot pork sausage meat
1 onion, chopped
1 litre carton chicken stock
2 425-g (15-ounce) cans stewed tomatoes
2 teaspoons (10 ml) chilli powder
1 green capsicum, seeded, chopped
2 cups black beans, soaked overnight

- Break up sausage and brown with onion in large frypan. Drain fat and transfer to large slow cooker.
- Add chicken stock, stewed tomatoes, capsicum, black beans and 1 cup (250 ml) water.
- Cover and cook on low for 3 to 4 hours. Serves 6.

Sausage Pizza Soup

455 g (16 ounces) Italian sausages, sliced
1 onion, chopped
2 115-g (4-ounce) cans sliced mushrooms
1 green capsicum, seeded, julienned
1 425-g (15-ounce) can Italian stewed tomatoes
½ litre carton beef stock
1 230-g (8-ounce) can pizza sauce

- Combine all ingredients in slow cooker and stir well.
- Cover and cook on low for 4 to 5 hours. Serves 6.

Pork-Vegetable Stew

455 g (1 pound) pork tenderloin
1 onion, coarsely chopped
1 red capsicum, seeded, julienned
455 g (16 ounces) frozen stew vegetables, thawed
2 tablespoons (15 g) flour
½ teaspoon dried rosemary leaves
½ teaspoon oregano leaves
½ litre carton chicken stock
170 g (6 ounces) long grain-wild rice

- Cut tenderloin into 2.5-cm (1-inch) cubes and brown in non-stick frypan.
- Place tenderloin in large sprayed slow cooker; add onion, capsicum and mixed vegetables.
- Stir flour, rosemary and oregano into ½ cup (125 ml) water in bowl and mix well. Pour this seasoning mixture and stock over vegetables.
- Cover and cook on low for 5 to 6 hours.
- When ready to serve, cook rice according to package directions.
- Serve pork and vegetables over rice. Serves 6.

You can buy sausage in several forms: fresh, cured, cooked, uncooked or dried. Read the labels carefully for cooking instructions.

Beans 'n Sausage Soup

455 g (1 pound) hot Italian sausage
1 onion, chopped
1 425-g (15-ounce) can Italian stewed tomatoes
1 cup black beans, soaked overnight
2 425-g (15-ounce) cans cannellini beans with liquid
1 litre carton beef stock
1 teaspoon minced garlic
1 teaspoon dried basil

- Cut sausage into 1.2-cm (½-inch) pieces.
- Brown sausage and onion in frypan, drain and transfer to 5 to 6-L (5 to 6-quart) slow cooker.
- Stir in tomatoes, black beans, cannellini beans, stock, garlic and basil and mix well.
- Cover and cook on low for 5 to 7 hours. Serves 6 to 8.

Italian Vegetable Stew

910 g (2 pounds) Italian sausage
2 455-g (16-ounce) frozen mixed vegetables
2 425-g (15-ounce) cans Italian stewed tomatoes
½ litre carton beef stock
1 teaspoon Italian seasoning
½ cup (40 g) pasta shells

- Brown sausage in frypan, cook for about 5 minutes and drain.
- Combine sausage, vegetables, stewed tomatoes, stock and Italian seasoning in 5 to 6-L (5 to 6-quart) slow cooker and mix well.
- Cover and cook on low for 3 to 5 hours.
- About 40 minutes before serving, add pasta to stew in slow cooker and cook until they are tender. Serves 8.

Recipes for the slow cooker were developed to make preparation as easy as possible because 'convenience products' such as seasoning mixes, sauce mixes and canned soups can be used in most recipes.

Southern Ham Stew

This is a great meal and it screams for cornbread.

2 cups (250 g) dried black-eyed peas
3 cups (420 g) cooked, cubed ham
1 large onion, chopped
2 cups (200 g) sliced celery
1 425-g (15-ounce) can chickpeas, drained
2 425-g (15-ounce) cans stewed tomatoes
½ litre carton chicken stock
2 tablespoons (15 g) cornflour

- Rinse and drain dried black-eyed peas and place in saucepan.
- Cover peas with water, bring to boil and drain again.
- Place peas in large slow cooker and add 5 cups (1.2 L) water, ham, onion, celery, chickpeas, tomatoes and stock.
- Cover and cook on low for 7 to 9 hours.
- Mix cornflour with ⅓ cup (75 ml) water in bowl, turn cooker to high, pour in cornflour mixture and stir well.
- Cook for about 10 minutes or until stew thickens.
- Add good amount of salt and pepper and stir well before serving. Serves 6 to 8.

TIP: If you would like a little spice in the stew, add 2 teaspoons of chilli powder.

Ham-Vegetable Chowder

When you bake a big ham, always make sure you have plenty leftover for this recipe.

1 medium potato
2 280-g (10-ounce) cans cream of celery soup
½ litre carton chicken stock
3 cups (420 g) cooked, finely diced ham
1 425-g (15-ounce) can corn kernels
2 carrots, peeled, sliced
1 onion, coarsely chopped
1 teaspoon dried basil
280 g (10 ounces) frozen broccoli florets

- Cut potato into 2.5-cm (1-inch) pieces.
- Combine all ingredients except broccoli with 1 teaspoon (5 ml) each of salt and pepper in large slow cooker.
- Cover and cook on low for 5 to 6 hours.
- Add broccoli and cook for additional 1 hour. Serves 8.

Ham and Cabbage Stew

2 425-g (15-ounce) cans Italian stewed tomatoes
3 cups (210 g) shredded cabbage
1 onion, chopped
1 red capsicum, seeded, chopped
2 tablespoons (30 g) butter
½ litre carton chicken stock
3 cups (420 g) cooked, diced ham
Cornbread

- Combine all ingredients plus ¾ teaspoon each of salt and pepper and 1 cup (250 ml) water in large slow cooker and mix well.
- Cover and cook on low for 5 to 7 hours. Great with cornbread. Serves 6.

Split Pea and Ham Chowder

1 medium potato, peeled
3 cups (420 g) cooked, cubed ham
455 g (16 ounces) dried split peas, rinsed
1 310-g (11-ounce) can corn kernels
½ litre carton chicken stock
2 carrots, sliced
2 sticks celery, diagonally sliced
1 tablespoon (15 ml) dried onion flakes
1 teaspoon dried marjoram leaves

- Cut potato into small cubes and place in sprayed slow cooker.
- Combine all ingredients plus 3 cups (750 ml) water and 1 teaspoon salt in slow cooker.
- Cover and cook on low for 6 to 8 hours. Serves 6 to 8.

Prawn and Chicken Jambalaya

4 boneless, skinless chicken breast halves, cubed
1 795-g (28-ounce) can diced tomatoes
1 onion, chopped
1 green capsicum, chopped
½ litre carton chicken stock
½ cup (125 ml) dry white wine
2 teaspoons dried oregano
2 teaspoons Cajun seasoning
½ teaspoon cayenne pepper
455 g (1 pound) cooked, peeled, veined prawns
2 cups (370 g) cooked rice

- Place all ingredients except prawns and rice in slow cooker and stir.
- Cover and cook on low for 6 to 8 hours.
- Turn heat to high, stir in prawns and rice and cook for additional 15 to 20 minutes. Serves 8.

Crab Chowder

2 small zucchini, thinly sliced
1 red capsicum, seeded, julienned
2 sticks celery, diagonally sliced
1 medium potato, peeled, cubed
2 tablespoons (30 g) butter, melted
1 cup chicken stock
2 tablespoons (15 g) cornflour
3 cups (750 ml) milk
2 170-g (6-ounce) cans crabmeat, drained, flaked
85 g (3 ounces) cream cheese, cubed

- Place zucchini, capsicum, celery, potato, butter, stock and 1 teaspoon salt in sprayed slow cooker.
- Stir cornflour into milk in bowl, stir and pour into slow cooker.
- Cover and cook on low for 3 to 4 hours.
- Turn heat to high, add crabmeat and cream cheese and stir until cream cheese melts. Serves 6.

Oyster Chowder

1 red capsicum, seeded, chopped
1 onion, chopped
½ litre carton chicken stock
1 medium potato, peeled, cubed
1 fresh jalapeno chilli, finely chopped
230 g (8 ounces) shucked fresh oysters with liquid
280 g (10 ounces) frozen corn kernels, thawed
1 teaspoon dried oregano
½ cup (125 ml) pouring cream

- Combine all ingredients except cream in slow cooker.
- Cover and cook on low for 3 to 4 hours.
- When ready to serve, stir in cream. Serves 4 to 6.

Beans and Barley Soup

2 420-g (15-ounce) cans borlotti beans with liquid
1½ litres chicken stock
½ cup (100 g) quick-cooking barley
1 425-g (15-ounce) can Italian stewed tomatoes

- Combine beans, stock, barley, stewed tomatoes and ½ teaspoon pepper in 6-L (6-quart) slow cooker and stir well.
- Cover and cook on low for 4 to 5 hours. Serves 4 to 6.

Italian Bean Soup

2 425-g (15-ounce) cans cannellini beans with liquid
2 425-g (15-ounce) cans borlotti beans with liquid
1 large onion, chopped
3 beef stock cubes
1 tablespoon (15 ml) minced garlic
2 teaspoons Italian seasoning
2 425-g (15-ounce) cans Italian stewed tomatoes
1 425-g (15-ounce) can cut green beans, drained

- Combine both cans of beans, onion, beef stock cubes, garlic, Italian seasoning and 2 cups (500 ml) water in large slow cooker.
- Cover and cook on low for 6 to 8 hours.
- Turn heat to high, add stewed tomatoes and green beans and stir well.
- Continue cooking for additional 30 minutes or until green beans are tender. Serves 6 to 8.

TIP: Serve with toasted focaccia.

French Onion Soup

5–6 onions, thinly sliced
1 clove garlic, minced
2 tablespoons (30 g) butter
1 litre carton beef stock
2 teaspoons Worcestershire sauce
6 2.5-cm (1-inch) slices bread
6 slices Swiss cheese

- Cook onions and garlic on low heat (do not brown) in hot butter in large frypan for about 20 minutes and stir several times.
- Transfer onion mixture to 4 to 5-L (4 to 5-quart) slow cooker.
- Add beef stock, Worcestershire sauce and 1 cup (250 ml) water.
- Cover and cook on low for 5 to 8 hours or on high for 2 hours 30 minutes to 3 hours.
- Before serving soup, toast bread slices and place cheese slice on top.
- Grill for 3 to 4 minutes or until cheese is light brown and bubbles.
- Ladle soup into bowls and top with toast. Serves 6.

Delicious Broccoli-Cheese Soup

455 g (16 ounces) frozen chopped broccoli florets, thawed
340 g (12 ounces) cubed cheddar cheese
30 g (1 ounce) white sauce mix
30 g (1 ounce) dry vegetable soup mix
1 340-g (12-ounce) can evaporated milk
½ litre carton chicken stock

- Combine all ingredients plus 2 cups (500 ml) water in large, sprayed slow cooker and stir well.
- Cover and cook on low for 6 to 7 hours or on high for 3 hours 30 minutes to 4 hours.
- Stir 1 hour before serving time. Serves 6.

Cheesy Potato Soup

6 medium potatoes, peeled, cubed
1 onion, very finely chopped
1 litre carton chicken stock
230 g (8 ounces) shredded Colby cheese
1 cup (250 ml) unthickened cream

- Combine potatoes, onion, chicken stock and ½ teaspoon pepper in slow cooker.
- Cover and cook on low for 8 to 10 hours.
- With potato masher, mash potatoes in slow cooker.
- About 1 hour before serving, stir in cheese and cream and cook for additional 1 hour. Serves 6.

Borlotti Bean-Vegetable Soup

4 425-g (15-ounce) cans borlotti beans with liquid
1 onion, chopped
1 red capsicum, chopped
1 green capsicum, chopped
2 cups (200 g) chopped celery
1 litre carton chicken stock
1 teaspoon Cajun seasoning

- Place all ingredients plus 1 cup (250 ml) water in 5-L (5-quart) slow cooker and stir well.
- Cover and cook on low for 5 to 6 hours. Serves 6.

TIP: If you want to give this soup a little 'kick', sprinkle a little cayenne or several drops of hot sauce. They will remember you that way.

The slow cooker has found new popularity with the busy lifestyle of today's cook. Not only is the slow cooker a time-saver, but it also saves energy because it uses very little electricity. When cooking on low, the slow cooker will use less energy than most light bulbs.

Creamy Vegetable Soup

1½ litres chicken stock
¼ cup (60 g) butter, melted
455 g (16 ounces) frozen mixed vegetables
1 onion, chopped
3 sticks celery, sliced
1 teaspoon ground cumin
3 zucchini, coarsely chopped
2 cups (140 g) chopped, fresh broccoli
1 cup (250 ml) unthickened cream

- Combine stock, butter, mixed vegetables, onion, celery, cumin, 1 teaspoon each of salt and pepper in large slow cooker and stir well.
- Cover and cook on low for 6 to 7 hours or on high for 3 to 4 hours.
- Stir in zucchini and broccoli. Cook for additional 30 minutes to 1 hour or until broccoli is tender but crisp.
- Turn off heat and stir in cream.
- Let stand for 10 minutes before serving. Serves 6.

The first cookbook published in America in 1742 in Williamsburg, Virginia, contained recipes for Soop Sante, Pease Soop, Craw Fish Soop, Brooth, and Soop with Teel, among others.

Pizza Soup

3 280-g (10-ounce) cans condensed tomato soup
1 280-g (10-ounce) can French onion soup
2 teaspoons Italian seasoning
¾ cup (55 g) tiny pasta shells
1½ cups (70 g) shredded mozzarella cheese

- Place both soups, Italian seasoning and 1½ soup cans water in 4 to 5-L (4 to 5-quart) slow cooker.
- Cook for 1 hour on high or until mixture is hot.
- Add pasta and cook for 1 hour 30 minutes to 2 hours or until pasta cooks. Stir several times to keep pasta from sticking to bottom of slow cooker.
- Turn heat off, add mozzarella cheese and stir until cheese melts. Serves 4.

TIP: If you want a special way to serve this soup, sprinkle some fried onions over top of each serving.

Soup with a Zip

2 425-g (15-ounce) cans stewed tomatoes
2 teaspoons chilli powder
1 litre carton chicken stock
2 280-g (10-ounce) cans chicken noodle soup
1 425-g (15-ounce) can corn kernels, drained
1 425-g (15-ounce) can cut green beans, drained
Shredded cheddar cheese

- Place all ingredients except cheese in 4 to 5-L (4 to 5-quart) slow cooker and mix well.
- Cover and cook on low for 2 to 3 hours.
- When ready to serve, sprinkle shredded cheese over each bowl of soup. Serves 6.

Minestrone Soup

2 425-g (15-ounce) cans Italian stewed tomatoes
910 g (16 ounces) frozen vegetables
2 cups cooked pasta
1½ litres beef stock
2 sticks celery, chopped
2 potatoes, peeled, cubed
1 teaspoon Italian herb seasoning
2 425-g (15-ounce) cans kidney beans, rinsed, drained
2 teaspoons minced garlic

- Combine all ingredients in large sprayed slow cooker and mix well.
- Cover and cook on low for 4 to 6 hours. Serves 8.

Pasta-Veggie Soup

2 yellow squash, chopped
2 zucchini, sliced
280 g (10 ounces) frozen corn, thawed
1 red capsicum, seeded, chopped
1 425-g (15-ounce) can stewed tomatoes
1 teaspoon Italian seasoning
2 teaspoons dried oregano
1 litre carton beef stock
¾ cup (55 g) small pasta shells

- Combine squash, zucchini, corn, capsicum, tomatoes, Italian seasoning, oregano, beef stock and 2 cups (500 ml) water in 6-L (6-quart) slow cooker.
- Cover and cook on low for 6 to 7 hours.
- Add pasta shells and cook for additional 30 to 45 minutes or until pasta is tender. Serves 4 to 6.

Vegetable-Lentil Soup

2 550-g (19-ounce) cans lentil soup
1 425-g (15-ounce) can stewed tomatoes
½ litre carton chicken stock
1 onion, chopped
1 green capsicum, chopped
3 sticks celery, sliced
1 carrot, halved, sliced
2 teaspoons minced garlic
1 teaspoon dried marjoram leaves

- Combine all ingredients in slow cooker and stir well.
- Cover and cook on low for 5 to 6 hours. Serves 4.

Vegetable Chilli

2 425-g (15-ounce) cans cannellini beans with liquid
1 425-g (15-ounce) can borlotti beans with liquid
2 425-g (15-ounce) cans stewed tomatoes
1 425-g (15-ounce) can corn kernels
1 onion, chopped
3 sticks celery, sliced
1 tablespoon (15 ml) chilli powder
2 teaspoons dried oregano leaves

- Combine cannellini beans, borlotti beans, tomatoes, corn, onion, celery, chilli powder, oregano, 1 teaspoon salt and 1½ cups (375 ml) water in 5 to 6-L (5 to 6-quart) slow cooker.
- Cover and cook on low for 4 to 6 hours. Serves 6.

Serious Bean Stew

455 g (16 ounces) smoked sausages
1 795-g (28-ounce) can baked beans with liquid
1 425-g (15-ounce) can cannellini beans with liquid
1 425-g (15-ounce) can borlotti beans with liquid
1 280-g (10-ounce) can French onion soup
1 onion, chopped
1 teaspoon Cajun seasoning
2 425-g (15-ounce) cans stewed tomatoes

- Peel skin from sausages and slice.
- Place in 6-L (6-quart) slow cooker, add remaining ingredients and stir to mix.
- Cover and cook on low for 3 to 4 hours.
- Serves 8.

Index

Q

R

S

W

Z